Jobs Gender and Small Enterprises in Africa

Ethiopian Women Entrepreneurs: Going for Growth

May 2003

**ILO Subregional Office, Addis Ababa, Ethiopia and
Women's Affairs Department, Ministry of Trade & Industry
(MTI/WAD)
in association with
InFocus Programme on Boosting Employment
through Small Enterprise Development
International Labour Office · Geneva**

ILO
Ethiopian Women Entrepreneurs: Going for Growth
Geneva, International Labour Office, 2003

ISBN 92-2-113753-8

Printed in Switzerland

Acknowledgements

Zewde & Associates PLC wish to express its profound gratitude to the ILO's InFocus Programme on Boosting Employment through Small Enterprise Development (IFP/SEED), and its team on Women's Entrepreneurship Development and Gender Equality (WEDGE) in particular, for offering the opportunity to undertake this research work, which was challenging and interesting.

Specifically, our appreciation goes to Mr. Gerry Finnegan, Senior Specialist in Women's Entrepreneurship Development in IFP/SEED, ILO Geneva, and to the ILO's international consultants, Ms. Rhona Howarth and Dr. Pat Richardson, for their valuable guidance and contributions to the outcome of this research.

Our thanks also go to W/ro Nigest Haile of the Women's Affairs Department of the Ministry of Trade and Industry of Ethiopia; Ms. Grania Mackie of the IFP/SEED's WEDGE unit and Mr. Urgessa Bedada, ILO Addis Ababa, for their important facilitation and support service.

Foreword

Within the Department of Job Creation and Enterprise Development (EMP/ENT), the InFocus Programme on Boosting Employment through Small Enterprise Development (IFP/SEED) is the ILO's major programme to promote employment creation for women and men through small enterprise development. IFP/SEED gives priority to a number of cross-cutting aspects, including "enhancing employment opportunities for women". IFP/SEED has a team engaged on Women's Entrepreneurship Development and Gender Equality (known as WEDGE), which has been conducting research on the theme of Jobs, Gender and Small Enterprises in Africa – specifically in Ethiopia, Tanzania and Zambia.

Throughout 2002 a comprehensive review was undertaken to examine the factors affecting women entrepreneurs in each of the three countries. The first stage involved recruiting teams of national consultants, commissioning research and conducting thorough literature reviews to capture the known facts regarding women entrepreneurs. This resulted in the publication of a set of three Preliminary Reports (October 2002) which summarized key findings from the secondary research and highlighted critical areas for further research. In Ethiopia, this research was conducted by Zewde & Associates. The next stage involved a field survey of 123 women entrepreneurs in Addis Ababa and 5 other urban centres, as well as 5 in-depth case studies, to dig deeper and probe these critical issues, particularly as they affect women entrepreneurs' motivations, economic opportunities and passages to growth and formalization. This process of formalization and the transition from the informal to the formal economy is of interest and concern to the ILO.

Once the field research was completed, a national conference was organized at which the significant survey findings were presented and possible interventions proposed. Resulting from the highly participatory consultative process at the national conference, a set of issues and recommendations for follow-up actions emerged. The Ethiopian conference was held in Addis Ababa on 19 November 2002. This report is the culmination of the research and consultations that took place throughout 2002, and it summarizes the key issues from the secondary research, describes and analyses the survey findings, and presents recommendations from the national consultative process.

In the Ethiopian study, the 123 women entrepreneurs included in the survey have created 852 jobs for themselves, their family and others, of which 596 are full-time paid jobs (an average of 4.8 per enterprise). Such significant job creation performance has occurred despite the financial, cultural and other disadvantages faced by women entrepreneurs in Ethiopia. Although many admit to accessing microfinance without any problems, just as larger enterprises are able to attract loans from commercial banks, when it comes to finding appropriate funds to finance business growth, there would appear to be a "missing middle" to finance the progression from informal to formal, and from micro-level to small and medium-scale enterprises. Therefore, the large majority (85 per cent) of the women entrepreneurs has had to depend on personal savings and family support for start-up finance. Therefore, the large majority (85 per cent) of the women entrepreneurs has had to depend on personal savings and family support for start-up finance. Issues of land title and lack of working premises featured prominently among the major barriers experienced by women entrepreneurs in establishing and growing their enterprises. Many of the women entrepreneurs complained of problems in finding or building their own working premises, and some 60 per cent have to rent at what they regard as a very high cost. Only five per cent of the women sell outside of their immediate local markets, therefore much has to be done to improve access to wider and more lucrative markets.

The entire research process conducted by the IFP/SEED's WEDGE team, and the final set of recommendations for practical actions, make a significant contribution towards the ILO's Jobs in Africa (JIA) programme and its Global Employment Agenda, particularly in relation to promoting gender equality and women's entrepreneurship as a positive "force of change". The evolving partnership with the Ministry of Trade and Industry, Women's Affairs Department (MTI/WAD), will ensure that the ILO's support to women's entrepreneurship makes a positive contribution to the implementation of the National Policy on Women, as well as to the implementation of the PRSP process in Ethiopia. The enhanced knowledge base on women entrepreneurs and the practical follow-up actions also contribute significantly to women's empowerment, as indicated in the Millennium Development Goals (Goal 3, Target 4, Indicator 11).

The Ethiopian research exercise has been conducted by Zewde & Associates under the leadership of Mr Zewde Biratu, on behalf of the ILO. The national research team was greatly assisted by the ILO's team of international consultants from Westfield Consultancy (Newcastle, UK), Ms Rhona Howarth and Dr. Pat Richardson. S/ro Nigest Haile, Head, MTI/WAD has been a strong supporter of the ILO's work on women's entrepreneurship over the past 2 years. Within the ILO, the research project was initiated, designed and supervised by Mr Gerry Finnegan, Senior Specialist in Women's Entrepreneurship Development, with assistance from Ms Grania Mackie (IFP/SEED). The ILO Subregional Office in Addis Ababa has supported this project during 2002, and valuable assistance has been provided by Mr Urgessa Bedada (Senior Programme Officer) and Ms Rahel Kebede (Senior Communications Assistant).

The ILO would like to acknowledge the financial support provided from the Irish Government under the ILO-Ireland Aid Partnership Programme, as well as the encouragement received from the Embassy of Ireland in Addis Ababa, and from the Charge d'Affaires, Ms Pauline Conway.

Michel Gozo
Director
ILO Subregional Office
Addis Ababa

Michael Henriques
Director
Job Creation and Enterprise
Development Department (EMP/ENT)
ILO, Geneva

Abstract

This report on "Ethiopian Women Entrepreneurs: Going for Growth" presents the conclusions and final set of recommendations based on outcomes from field research and a national conference organized by the ILO. The field research covered 123 women entrepreneurs from Addis Ababa and five other major cities, as well as in-depth interviews with five other women entrepreneurs. The final recommendations are the result of a consultative process undertaken at the ILO's National Symposium on Women Entrepreneurs in Ethiopia, held in November 2002.

The 123 women entrepreneurs included in the survey have created 852 jobs for themselves, their family and others, of which 596 are full-time paid jobs (an average of 4.8 per enterprise). Such significant performance in job creation has occurred despite the financial, cultural and other disadvantages faced by women entrepreneurs in Ethiopia. Although many admit to accessing microfinance without any problems, just as larger enterprises are able to attract loans from commercial banks, when it comes to finding appropriate funds to finance business growth, there would appear to be a "missing middle" to finance the progression from informal to formal, and from micro-level to small and medium-scale enterprises. Therefore, the large majority (85 per cent) of the women had to depend on personal savings and family support for start-up finance. Consequently, the large majority (85 per cent) of the women entrepreneurs invested personal savings and family resources for start-up finance. Issues of land title and lack of working premises featured prominently among the major barriers experienced by women entrepreneurs in establishing and growing their enterprises. Many of the women entrepreneurs complained of problems in finding or building their own working premises, and some 60 per cent have to rent at what they regard as a very high cost. Only five per cent of the women sell outside of their immediate local markets, therefore much has to be done to improve access to wider and more lucrative markets.

Associations of women entrepreneurs in Ethiopia are still a new phenomenon, and most of the associations are both young and lacking in capacity. However, with the support of the MTI/WAD and the donor community, the associations could become stable and eventually be commercially sustainable, representative organizations playing a key role in providing support for their members.

Acronyms

AEMFI	Association of Ethiopian Micro-finance Institutions
BDS	Business Development Service
COMESA	Common Market for Eastern and Southern Africa
CSA	Central Statistical Agency
FeMSEDA	Federal Micro and Small Enterprises Development Agency
GDP	Gross Domestic Product
GNP	Gross National Product
GTZ	German Technical Cooperation
IGA	Income Generating Activity
ILO	International Labour Organization
MEDAC	Ministry of Economic Development and Cooperation
MFI	Micro-finance Institution(s)
MSE	Micro and Small Enterprise(s)
NGO	Non-Government Organization(s)
PRSP	Poverty Reduction Strategic Paper
ReMSEDA	Regional Micro and Small Enterprises Development Agency(ies)
TITB	Trade Industry and Tourism Bureau(x)
TOT	Training of Trainers
WAD	Women Affairs Department(s)
WDF	Women Development Fund
WEA	Women Entrepreneurs' Association(s)
WED	Women's Entrepreneurship Development
WEF	Women Exporters' Forum
WEPC	Women's Enterprise Promotion Centre
WEDGE	Women's Entrepreneurship Development and Gender Equality

Table of Contents

Executive Summary

I. Introduction

This report is the culmination of a research process initiated by the ILO in Ethiopia at the beginning of 2002. It presents the findings of primary field research conducted with 123 women entrepreneurs, and in particular on the factors that facilitate or inhibit the growth of their businesses. The Ethiopian research was part of a larger exercise by the ILO, funded as part of the ILO-Ireland Aid Partnership Programme, under IFP/SEED's Jobs, Gender and Small Enterprises in Africa project. The ILO commissioned studies in three countries – namely, Ethiopia, Tanzania and Zambia – to identify factors affecting women entrepreneurs. The studies were conducted through two key phases of work, with the first phase being desk-based secondary research to review the literature on enterprise development and women's entrepreneurship in each country. From this research a set of preliminary reports, Jobs, Gender and Small Enterprises: Factors Affecting Women Entrepreneurs in Micro and Small Enterprises (MSEs) in each of the three designated countries was produced. The preliminary report on Ethiopia was published by the ILO in 2002, and distributed widely both nationally and internationally (Zewde & Associates, 2002).

In the Ethiopian context, the secondary research helped to clarify the key questions to be addressed through the primary research, and also identified the sample group: women who had been operating a micro and small enterprise for more than two years, and who have licences in their own names. The field research was conducted between April and August 2002. From across 6 urban areas in Ethiopia, 123 women entrepreneurs were interviewed on a one-to-one basis, and five case studies were developed to illustrate the women entrepreneurs' experiences in a more in-depth manner.

The primary research was intended to explore critical issues that were identified by the secondary research, and to recommend practical actions to assist women entrepreneurs in micro and small enterprises, with the ultimate aim of improving the development of women's entrepreneurship in Ethiopia. This report describes who the women are who run formal enterprises in Ethiopia; the types of enterprises they are engaged in; the challenges they face, and the lessons that can be drawn from their experiences of setting up and growing businesses. In addition, this report includes a number of the consultants' proposed actions that would support women entrepreneurs in Ethiopia to build successful businesses and create meaningful employment, and ultimately contribute to the reduction of poverty.

The findings from the fieldwork and the accompanying consultants' proposals were then brought forward to a national conference that took place in November 2002. At the national conferences, participants were asked to take account of the results of the primary research and to consider the consultants' set of proposals (as presented in the "proposed interventions" at the end of this report). Following participatory consultations at the national conference, a list of key issues, priorities and recommendations was compiled. The outcomes from the Addis Ababa conference (19 November 2002), which was attended by more than 140 women entrepreneurs and key actors, are summarized below. This conference and the related participatory consultative process comprised the third stage of the ILO's research project in Ethiopia.

The production of this final report, which includes the set of revised findings from the primary research, the consultants' set of proposed interventions, and the outcomes from the national conference, makes up the final stage of the ILO's research process on women entrepreneurs in Ethiopia.

In summary, the key survey findings show that the major motivating factors for women starting their own businesses are to support their families, to be self-employed and to generate their own income. Nearly 70 per cent of the women entrepreneurs currently engaged in small-scale enterprises had started as microenterprises and had grown their businesses over time, and 66 per cent of the women entrepreneurs surveyed had expanded and/or diversified their businesses to some degree since establishment.

The research also identified that the 123 micro and small enterprises provide jobs for others and employed a total of 825 persons, of which 75 per cent were employed by small-scale enterprises and 25 per cent by microenterprises. These are two key factors that contradict commonly held perceptions of women-owned and managed enterprises as having little growth potential and being unable to offer real sustainable employment.

The survey indicated that the main resources for start-up and expansion of women-operated enterprises come from the women's own personal savings and family support. Whilst this might be a strength at start-up, it was felt to be a constraint for the women when they were trying to mobilize adequate working capital and plan for the expansion of their businesses. Savings alone were not always sufficient for running and expanding the business, and many felt that there is a need for additional credit that is appropriate to the needs of a growing business.

Women entrepreneurs also expressed the view that they find it very difficult to access credit from banks due to the fact that they often do not have access to the type or levels of collateral required by the banks. Credit through Micro-Finance Institutions (MFIs) also presents difficulties in that MFIs were not always able to meet the credit requirements of the businesses, i.e. they offer limited loan sizes and short repayment terms.

In terms of business development support, the primary research showed that the women entrepreneurs mainly depend on their own skills and experience, as well as drawing support from family and friends when starting up and expanding their businesses. The women entrepreneurs' use of external formal support was very limited.

II.   Summary of Major Findings

The primary research provided a broad range of information on women entrepreneurs and women-operated enterprises, and on the problems and opportunities facing women entrepreneurs in Ethiopia. The research has also contributed to a greater understanding and knowledge of the experiences of women's business growth, the business support framework, and the broader environment within which women's businesses operate in Ethiopia. The following are the major findings arising from the fieldwork investigations, and these are presented in more detail in section 5.

(i)   Regional Divergence

Although the survey was carried out in six different major towns of six regional states, including Addis Ababa, there was little difference in the way the women start and develop their businesses or in the overall enabling or support environment, apart from Addis Ababa, which is the capital city, whose population is larger and therefore offers greater market opportunities.

(ii)   General Characteristics of the Women Entrepreneurs and their Enterprises

The majority of women entrepreneurs (87 per cent) are less than 49 years of age; 89 per cent were married, divorced or widowed, and most have attained secondary levels of schooling. The average household size was found to be 6 persons.

The research confirmed that the major motivating factors for women to start their own businesses were to support their families, to be self-employed, and to generate their own income. The survey results showed that 44 per cent are engaged in services, 30 per cent in trade, 15 per cent in production, and the remaining 11 per cent in both trade and handicrafts. It was also observed that they have created employment opportunities for themselves and others. The 123 women-owned enterprises in the sample have created a total of 825 jobs (average of 6.7 per enterprise), of which 592 are full-time jobs (average 4.8 per enterprise).

(iii)   Financial and Non-Financial Resources

a. Financial Resources

The main financial sources for the start-up and expansion of women-operated enterprises came from personal savings and family loans/contributions. This has proved to be a constraint for some women entrepreneurs, especially when trying to mobilize capital for expanding or diversifying the business. Many women entrepreneurs reported that savings alone were not sufficient for running and expanding their businesses. Therefore, the growth of the enterprises is restricted due to lack of finance for working capital and investments. The women entrepreneurs found it very difficult to access credit from banks due to the requirements of the banks, such as the collateral, the expected level of contribution from the women entrepreneurs themselves, and from MFIs due to the low loan ceiling, and the inconvenient lending and repayment arrangements.

b. Non-Financial Resources

The majority of women entrepreneurs (60 per cent) experienced difficulties in finding land and premises for production or provision of services, as well as for selling purposes. Most run their businesses from rented premises, but the relatively high rents poses critical problems for them and can hinder their expansion and diversification.

The vast majority of women entrepreneurs market their products and services to their local market, which for most means a limited market access. Because of these reasons, many of the women entrepreneurs are engaged in stiff competition with each another for the same small local market, and this inevitably results in lower returns all round. The potential for market development is limited since many women are engaged in similar types of businesses. Many any of these business sectors are traditionally dominated by women for traditional and socio-cultural reasons. The mobility of some of the women entrepreneurs is restricted by family responsibilities and cultural barriers, and this also contrives to limit their access to wider markets.

Most of the women entrepreneurs sell their products directly to consumers, and few market through intermediaries such as wholesalers. The limited linkages between the women micro-entrepreneurs and the medium and large businesses also mean that their opportunities are limited for networking and growth.

Women entrepreneurs use a narrow range of promotional methods with the majority use word of mouth and signboards to advertise their products/services. Many women entrepreneurs lack access to adequate business development services (BDS), although organizations such as WISE, GTZ, UNIDO and Enterprise Ethiopia, as well as the ILO, are redoubling their efforts in this regard. There seems to be only a limited range of services available that are tailored to the specific needs of women entrepreneurs.

(iv)   Managerial Capacity of the Women Entrepreneurs

Many women entrepreneurs manage their enterprises with support from family and friends, both at start-up and expansion. Use of external, formal, managerial capacity-building support by women entrepreneurs is very limited.

(v)   Networking

The women entrepreneurs' associations are mainly young organizations, and at present they do not appear to be very strong and do not meet the full range of needs of the women entrepreneurs. Membership levels are low and some of the women entrepreneurs do not feel that there would be real benefits from joining.

(vi)   Decision-Making

The majority of women entrepreneurs make their own independent decisions on the utilization of money generated from their businesses, as well as on matters that affect their business. A significant number of the women surveyed who operate small enterprises make joint decisions with their husbands when the decision involves complex matters or where the husband's permission is required – for example offering their joint property as collateral or disposing of a major property.

(vii)   Awareness Level of Government Policies

There appears to be an adequate level of awareness among women entrepreneurs about government policies that concern their businesses. However, most of the women entrepreneurs think that changes are required to create a more conducive environment for their respective operations and to facilitate the growth of their enterprises. In particular, most have mentioned that the tax system needs a significant improvement, as the existing tax laws, which now levy taxes on the basis of estimates, do not consider the ability of small businesses to pay taxes.

(viii) Differences between Micro and Small Enterprises

As far as access to resources or support services is concerned, both the micro and small enterprise categories seem to face the same constraints at start-up and during the growth stage of their enterprises.

III. Recommendations from the ILO's Research on Women Entrepreneurs in Ethiopia

Section 6 of the report presents a set of proposals for supportive interventions, as prepared by the national consultants, Zewde & Associates. These interventions were introduced at the ILO's national conference on women entrepreneurs, held in Addis Ababa on 19 November 2002. The conference was attended by approximately 140 key actors and women entrepreneurs. Participants deliberated on the consultants' proposed interventions and came up with a final list which included 4 sets of recommendations.   These recommendations, resulting from the participatory consultative process during the national conference, are shown in detail in section 7 of this report. These recommendations will inform ILO's present and future actions in support of women entrepreneurs in Ethiopia, as well as in its evolving partnership with MTI/WAD.

(a) Access to Resources, in particular to Finance

I. There is a need to strengthen the capacities of MFIs in order that they are better able to:
- Extend their activities to more women as well as a wider range of women entrepreneurs;
- Improve the coverage of their services across the country;
- Improve their products and lending services to meet the needs of growth-oriented businesswomen by providing larger loans and longer repayment periods;
- Review interest rates with a view to offering variable rates based on business needs.

II. The Government should give special emphasis to the allocation of land and premises to women entrepreneurs at reasonable rates.

III. Where market failure exists, SME development incubators need to be established to help alleviate the shortage of appropriate premises for women entrepreneurs, as well as the provision of more and better BDS and information services for women entrepreneurs.

(b) Market Access and Developing BDS

I. In the face of apparent market failure, BDS providers should consider offering assistance in marketing to facilitate women entrepreneurs' access to local, regional and international markets, and to encourage and promote the greater use of technology to achieve this.

II. The ILO should continue with its support for improving market access for women entrepreneurs through trade fairs, and continue promoting international lessons and best practices.

III. The Government and business advocacy groups should encourage links between BDS providers, MFIs and other financial institutions to improve women entrepreneurs' access to the full range of financial and non-financial (BDS) support services available.

IV. BDS products and services should be promoted to move women entrepreneurs into more profitable sectors and to help make their enterprises more productive and competitive. This should involve BDS provision in areas such as:
- Quality assurance schemes
- Productivity Improvement Programmes
- Production technology
- Product development
- Packaging development
- Business skills development
- Information about markets including export markets
- Support with information technology

(c) Capacity Building for BDS

I. A review is needed of the existing provision of business support services (BDS): who provides BDS, and what is the current market situation for BDS in Ethiopia with particular reference to women entrepreneurs' access to and take-up/use of BDS.

II. Improve women entrepreneurs' access to resources by, for example, encouraging associations of women entrepreneurs to help their members to access BDS through referral systems.

III. Develop capacities and capabilities of BDS providers in areas such as networking, lobbying, empowerment, gender equality issues, and decision-making for women entrepreneurs.

IV. BDS providers can encourage the greater uptake of their services through cost-sharing initiatives (with WEAs and other organizations) and by providing demand-driven services.

V. BDS providers should promote the provision of integrated support across the MSE sector, and for women entrepreneurs in particular, that meets a range of client needs and avoids duplication, rather than offering a range of *ad hoc* provision of BDS.

VI. While developing more extensive and better BDS provision throughout the country, the financial sustainability of the BDS services should be a priority.

(d)   Enabling Environment

I. As the informal economy is largely dominated by women, it is important that steps are taken by the Government and BDS providers to improve their economic and social protection position by:
   - Providing some form of 'official' recognition to informal workers to protect them from harassment and provide basic forms of social protection;
   - Providing financial and non-financial support to women in the informal economy so that they can more easily access and navigate the steps involved in formalizing their businesses.

II. The Government should take the lead in a number of initiatives aimed at changing the attitudes of society towards women entrepreneurs and creating a more positive and constructive environment for their expansion and growth.

III. Special efforts should be made to improve partnerships between all actors who influence the socio-economic environment for women in general, and for women entrepreneurs in particular. This could be done within the framework of the PRSP process, and under the umbrella of the Women's Affairs Division, Office of the Prime Minister.

IV. There is a need to promote and support the practice of good governance by all, in Government, business and non-government organizations. There is a need to highlight and reward positive, honest and transparent practices wherever and whenever they occur.

V. There is a need to promote gender equality in enterprise development through:
   - Enforcing laws in an equitable and transparent manner
   - Identifying and promoting the dissemination of good practice examples from other countries
   - Promoting women entrepreneur role models through videos films and other publicity and promotional materials.

VI. Develop women entrepreneurs' voice through advocacy and lobbying. Women entrepreneurs need to be supported and profiled in exercising their rights.

1. Introduction

1.1 Background

Throughout the world it is acknowledged that micro and small enterprises play a vital role in socio-economic development as a means for generating sustainable employment and incomes. Furthermore, the informal economy is increasingly being recognized by governments and donors as an important part of the wider economy in that it provides the breeding ground for micro and small enterprises, and in the process contributing to the reduction of poverty.

Women account for the larger share of the informal economy operators, as well as those running micro and small enterprises in Ethiopia. MSEs make a significant contribution to the socio-economic life of the country by way of supporting people to earn money and make a contribution to family incomes, and by supplying basic goods and services for local consumption. However, this contribution is not fully recognized or understood, and there is little in the way of research or statistics to provide a broader understanding of women's experience as business owners, their contribution to economic development, or the challenges they face in setting up, managing and growing their enterprises.

Women entrepreneurs face and deal with a diverse range of challenges and problems on a day-to-day basis, and these have hampered their growth and the potential contributions they could make towards creating meaningful and sustainable employment and a vibrant small business base.

In order to identify and implement strategic actions to support the development and growth of women's enterprises, the ILO, in partnership with Ireland Aid, as part of the InFocus Programme on Boosting Employment through Small Enterprise Development (IFP/SEED), commissioned a Women's Entrepreneurship Development (WED) research project in three countries – Ethiopia, Tanzania and Zambia.

The overall aim of the WED project is to:

> *Identify ways in which governments, the ILO, donors, NGOs and private sector can improve the prospects for women's entrepreneurship in the three designated countries and enhance the contribution of women entrepreneurs to the creation of meaningful and sustainable employment opportunities and poverty alleviation and reduction.*

The three-country approach to the project adds value to the understanding of women's enterprise in Africa, and has allowed for comparisons and similarities of experiences between countries to be explored. These comparative aspects will be further developed in a synthesis report, being prepared for ILO's IFP/SEED by the two international consultants engaged in this process, Ms. Rhona Howarth and Dr. Pat Richardson, from Westfield Consultancy, U.K.

This research project on Jobs, Gender and Small Enterprises in Africa was carried out through two phases of work. The secondary research phase was a desk-based exercise looking at existing research and literature in each country to gain a broader understanding of the status of women's enterprise, the support environment, and the challenges for women's enterprise. The secondary research work identified key factors affecting women entrepreneurs and their business development in Ethiopia, and shaped the focus of the primary research work, including the questions to be addressed, and helped identify the target group to be selected for the fieldwork.

1.2 Country Context

Ethiopia, with an area of 1.3 million square kilometers, has a population of about 63 million growing at an average of 2.8 per cent per year. However, because of structural problems, natural and man-made crises, the country has been characterized as backward. The GNP per capita of US $ 167 per annum (1999) is one of the lowest in the world. The majority of the population lies below the poverty line. Health services cover only 45 per cent of the population. The adult literacy rate in 1995 according to Ministry of Economic Development and Cooperation (MEDAC) was 35.5 per cent. The combined ratio of enrolment at primary, secondary and tertiary levels was only 17 per cent – much lower than the average for sub-Saharan Africa of 42 per cent.

The agricultural sector, consisting mostly of peasant farms, accounts for roughly 51.4 per cent of the GDP, 85 per cent of total employment and 90 per cent of export earnings (MEDAC, 1997). The manufacturing sector plays a less significant role as compared to agriculture. The major manufacturing sectors are food, beverages, textiles, clothing and leather.

The Federal Government of Ethiopia has adopted a free market economic policy and a development strategy known as Agricultural Led Industrialization (ADLI). This includes four key components, namely maintenance of an appropriate macroeconomic framework; improvements in agricultural efficiency and growth; private sector development and reform of public sector, and alleviation of poverty and development of human resources.

The Poverty Reduction Strategy Paper (PRSP) has been adopted after significant consultation between Government, private sector, NGOs, donors and civil society in order to address the real problems and constraints facing the country. The incorporation of women's entrepreneurship development problems in the strategy would certainly facilitate the socio-economic empowerment of women.

Along with the overall development policy and strategy, different policies and measures have been undertaken to promote the development of the country. MSEs comprise the lion's share of the number of establishments and jobs in the non-agricultural sectors, and are also the focus of Government's attention. Particularly, considering the important role that MSEs play in creating income and employment opportunities and eventually as a tool for poverty reduction, the Federal Government developed a strategy for the development and promotion of MSEs in 1997.

1.3 The Micro and Small Enterprise (MSE) Sector in Ethiopia

The secondary research provided an overview of the size and diversity of the MSE sector in Ethiopia. In particular, a survey conducted by the Central Statistical Authority (CSA) in May 1997 in 48 major towns showed that there are 584,913 informal sector activity operators and 2,731 small-scale manufacturing industries that give employment to 739,898 in the labour force.

The survey revealed that a microenterprise on an average engages one person, and the average annual operating surplus is about Birr 1,300. Regarding the diversity of the informal sector (microenterprises), the secondary research indicated that a large number of informal sector operators are concentrated in a limited number of business sectors and activities: 47 per cent are in manufacturing; 42 per cent in Trade, Hotel and Restaurant activities; about 6 per cent in Community and Personal services, and the rest (5 per cent) are involved in Agriculture, Hunting, Forestry and Fishing, Mining and Quarrying, Construction and Transport activities.

On the other hand, the CSA survey on Small Scale Manufacturing Industries showed that the small manufacturing industries are mainly engaged in the manufacture of food, fabricated metal, furniture, and clothing. These sectors constitute more than 85 per cent of the surveyed small-scale manufacturing industries. The small-scale manufacturing sector engages on average 3 persons (including owners) per enterprise, and the average employee per micro-level industrial enterprise is 2 persons.

The MSE sector is characterized by highly diversified activities, which can create job opportunities for a substantial segment of the population. This indicates that the sector can be a quick remedy for any unemployment problem. To curb unemployment and facilitate the environment for new job seekers and self-employment, a direct intervention and support by the Government is crucial. Hence, in order to assist in channelling the support to this diversified sector, definitions will be needed to help to categorize the sector accordingly.

According to the CSA (1997) Survey, 59 per cent of women entrepreneurs were illiterate, while nearly 20 per cent had an elementary formal education (grade 1-6) background. The survey also revels that 87 per cent of women entrepreneurs are married, divorced and widowed compared to 69.8 per cent of their male counterparts. This tends to show that often women become entrepreneurs in order to support their family because of the responsibilities they shoulder as married women, as well as due to the problems they face when they are divorced and widowed.

1.4   The Primary Research Approach

1.4.1 Key Questions

At the conclusion of the secondary study (Zwede and Associates, 2002), the following key questions were identified as being the focus of the primary research:

- Why are the majority of Ethiopian women entrepreneurs engaged in and apparently confined to informal enterprises, which are vulnerable?
- What lessons can be drawn from the experiences of women in growing their businesses?
- What measures could be taken to promote/support Ethiopian women entrepreneurs engaged in small-scale enterprises?

In addition, and in order to meet the overall aims of the WED study, the survey sought to draw out issues of gender relating to attitudes, laws, customs, practices and expectations, and to measure the extent to which these impact upon women and their enterprises.

1.4.2 Survey Sample

It was never intended that the study sample should be statistically representative of women entrepreneurs in Ethiopia. The purpose of the study was to examine a number of those women entrepreneurs engaged in running and growing registered businesses, to examine their experiences, and to draw lessons that could be relevant to the support of women's enterprise in Ethiopia. Such women entrepreneurs involved in running and growing registered businesses are likely to be exceptions to the majority of women business owners in Ethiopia. The target group for the field survey was identified as a result of the secondary research, and was agreed as being women who had been through a process of business growth, or that they had tried to grow their businesses. In agreeing on this sample group, it was noted that most of these women entrepreneurs were likely to be based in urban areas. To summarize, it was agreed between the team of national consultants (Zewde & Associates), the ILO's international consultants (Rhona Howarth and Pat Richardson), and the ILO's WEDGE team, that the focus of the study should be on urban women entrepreneurs who had been formally operating micro and small enterprises for at least 6 months, and who were registered and/or had licences in their names, and had majority ownership of their businesses. The sectors included in the study were production, services and trade.

1.4.3 Survey Instruments

The research was conducted through a survey comprising one-to-one interviews using both structured and unstructured questions (see Annex 1). The questionnaire was designed to focus on various aspects of the woman entrepreneur herself; the characteristics of her enterprise; the processes that she has gone through in starting and growing her enterprise; the broader enabling environment within which she operates, and the impact that the broader socio/economic context has on the woman and her enterprise.

The national study team, Zewde & Associates, who were assisted by field workers from the respective regional towns, undertook the survey. Training was given to the field workers and guidelines prepared in local language to enhance the interview process. One-to-one discussions were conducted with women entrepreneurs, and the average time taken for the discussion was two hours per enterprise, without taking into consideration the travel time between enterprises and the repeat visits made to meet the women entrepreneurs for the interviews.

1.4.4 Definitions Used

Given that the language of enterprise can sometimes be unclear and that there are no universally applied definitions, it was agreed that working definitions should be adopted for the field survey (primary research) as follows:

- Formal Enterprises are those registered and licensed by the respective Federal/ Regional Trade and Tourism Bureau and with an asset value of more than Birr 5,000 (USD 588);

- Microenterprises are those registered or licensed by the respective Regional Trade and Tourism Bureaux, employing more than 2 people and with assets valued between Birr 10,000 - 20,000 (USD1,176 - 2,353).

- Small Enterprises are those registered and licensed by the respective Federal/ Regional Bureaux, employing more than 5 people, and with assets valued between Birr 20,000 - 500,000 (USD 2,353 – 58,824).

In addition, the following commonly used terms were clarified:
- Trade is defined as buying and selling of commodities and merchandise.
- Services are defined as intangible business activities such hairdressing, catering services, etc.
- Production is defined as the process of transforming inputs into outputs of goods, mostly by manufacturing processes.
- Growth-oriented enterprises are those enterprises who have operated for more than two years, and have shown increases in their sales (revenue), capital, employment and products/services, as well as expansion and/or diversification in their businesses.

1.4.5 Sample Survey

Surveys were undertaken in selected towns by use of the questionnaire (see Annex 1). During the survey, 123 women entrepreneurs were identified and interviewed on a one-to-one basis. Case studies were prepared to highlight five women entrepreneurs (two from micro and three from small-scale enterprise as role models), selected from Addis Ababa. The five women entrepreneurs are additional to those covered by the sample survey. The case studies were prepared as the result of an intensive in-depth interview and discussions with each of the women entrepreneurs.

As shown in Table 1, the survey was carried out in 6 regional towns of Ethiopia, i.e. Addis Ababa, Nazareth, Awassa, Bahir Dar, Mekelle and Dire Dawa, which are the major towns where the majority of women entrepreneurs are operating. In the field survey, 123 women entrepreneurs were interviewed in the proportion of 55 per cent micro-level entrepreneurs and 45 per cent small entrepreneurs.

Table 1:   Distribution of Surveyed Enterprises by Type and Selected Towns

Town of interview	Type of Enterprise		Total
	Micro	Small	
Addis Ababa	10	10	20
Awassa	11	11	22
Bahir Dar	13	8	21
Dire Dawa	9	11	20
Mekelle	15	5	20
Nazareth	10	10	20
Total	68 55.3%	55 44.7%	123 100.0%

1.4.6 Overview of the Study Areas

The following six major towns including Addis Ababa, constituted the focus of the planned assessment of the constraints faced by women entrepreneurs in the country.

Addis Ababa – This is the capital city of Ethiopia and the seat of the Federal Government. According to the CSA's population projection of 1994, its population was 2.8 million in 2001. Out of the total population, about 51.8 per cent are women. Merkato, one of the biggest open market in Africa, is found in Addis Ababa. In addition to Merkato, Addis Ababa has big open markets along four of its major routes to other regional states. In these open markets, which are held twice a week, people living in Addis Ababa and its peripheries meet to exchange their products and services.

Dire Dawa – Located about 515 kilometres to the east of Addis Ababa, Dire Dawa is the second largest city. It is situated in a strategic location between Addis Ababa and Djibouti along the railway line. It is home for several different ethnic groups.

Bahir Dar – It is the capital city of the Amhara National Regional State, where business activities including micro and small enterprises are increasingly becoming very important. As a result, Bahir Dar is one of the major towns in the region, as well as in the country as a whole, where a large number of MSE operators exist and potential new ones could flourish.

Awassa – It is the seat of the Southern Nations, Nationalities and Peoples Regional State, located in the southern part of the country. According to the 1997 CSA statistics, Awassa is the major town in the Region where a high concentration of MSE operators exist. It is located in one of the tourist attraction areas, and a number of small-scale enterprises engaged in tourism-related services are flourishing.

Mekelle – It is the seat of the Northern Regional State, Tigray. Mekelle being a political as well as business centre of the Tigray Region, a number of business establishments are operational, ranging from micro to large-scale basic industries.

Nazareth – It is located 100 kilometres south of Addis Ababa. It is a Regional State seat of Oromia and its location – being close to Addis and on the route of the Ethio-Djibouti railway line – has made it an important business town. Nazareth is also located at a centre connecting the three regions and administrative councils of Dire Dawa, Southern Region and Addis Ababa. Thus, a number of MSE-related manufacturing and service activities are concentrated there.

1.4.7 The Structure of the Report

The remainder of the report comprises five sections. These include profiling the women entrepreneurs, their enterprises and their experiences of growing their businesses; examining these experiences in more depth through the five case studies; highlighting the key conclusions and proposed interventions from the research, and finally reporting on the recommendations arising from the stakeholder conference.

2. Profile of the Women Entrepreneurs and their Enterprises

As noted above, the aim of the primary research was to look at a particular group of women entrepreneurs in Ethiopia, i.e. those who had been in business for some time, had formalized their businesses and appeared to be growing their businesses – and to learn from their experience and see if lessons could be gained to help Ethiopian women entrepreneurs in general to grow sustainable businesses. So the research investigated questions such as, "Who are these women entrepreneurs and what are their businesses?", and "Are they typical of the profile of Ethiopian women entrepreneurs presented by other research?"

2.1 Characteristics of the Women Entrepreneurs

2.1.1 Age of the Women Entrepreneurs

In terms of age, the survey findings are summarized in Table 2 which indicates that over 89 per cent the women entrepreneurs interviewed were under the age of 50, with a fairly even spread of different age groups represented in each of the different study areas. Out of these, the majority (62 per cent) are in the group of 20-39, showing that most of the women interviewed are potentially of an age where they are economically active and also likely to be involved in undertaking family care responsibilities as wives, mothers and daughters.

Table 2: Age of Respondents by the Town of Interview

| Age bracket | Town of Interview | | | | | | Total | % |
	Addis Ababa	Awassa	Bahir Dar	Dire Dawa	Mekele	Nazareth		
Less than 20	-	-	2	-	-	1	3	2.4
20 – 39	9	11	16	11	15	14	76	61.8
40 – 49	8	10	1	4	5	3	31	25.2
50 –59	3	1	2	4	-	1	11	8.9
60 – above	-	-	-	1	-	-	2	1.6
Total	20	22	21	20	20	20	123	100.0

The predominance of women entrepreneurs in the age group 20 to 39 could be due to a number of things: lack of alternative employment opportunities in the formal employment sectors; the need to generate income either as the primary earner for the household or in a supplementary role, or simply the wish to own their own business. The background to and motivation for business ownership are discussed in more depth later in the report, but at this point it is noted that many (49 per cent) of the women interviewed were not employed prior to becoming entrepreneurs, describing themselves economically as students, housewives or unemployed (Table 5). A further 16 per cent had been engaged in another business prior to starting their current business.

2.1.2 Marital Status

Previous studies in Ethiopia have shown that the majority of women business owners are or have been married (Zewde & Associates, 2002), and this was also the case for this study, with nearly 80 per cent of the women interviewed falling into this category (as shown in Table 3). Out of these women entrepreneurs, 60 per cent of micro entrepreneurs and 69 per cent of small-scale women entrepreneurs are married, which in Ethiopian society brings with it family care responsibilities. In terms of the size of the businesses, slightly more married women are operating small (69 per cent) than microenterprises (60 per cent), with the reverse being the case for single women. Single women make up 28 per cent of the microenterprises in the sample, and 13 per cent of the small enterprises.

These differences may indicate that for women who start business at a micro level, it can take some time before the business has grown to the level of a small enterprise, and by that time most women have married. Women who directly go into small enterprises appear to be those who had the opportunity to use their parents' houses as production premises or as collateral to borrow from banks. From the five case studies, Semret with her bakery business and Romane with her printing press business are good examples of such women.

The numbers of single women in microenterprises may be as a result of the acute problem of unemployment in the country, with young women resorting to self-employment. The case study of Belainesh, a young woman of 24 who dropped out of school at grade ten and started tailoring school, is such an example.

Table 3: Marital Status of the Women Entrepreneurs

Marital Status	Frequency	%
Married	78	63.4
Divorced	5	4.1
Separated	1	0.8
Single	26	21.1
Widowed	13	10.6
Total	**123**	**100.0**

Widowed women in the sample are represented in both groups of enterprises, with 10 per cent of micro and 11 per cent of small enterprises who are widows.

2.1.3 Household Size

The average national household size in Ethiopia according to the most recent Government surveys is 4.8 persons (CSA, 1995). The average (both mean and median) household size of the women entrepreneurs surveyed was 6 persons. Three of the women stated that they were living with one other person, whilst at the other end of the spectrum one woman reported belonging to a household of 15 persons. There appears to be little relationship between household size and the size of the business, the average household size for micro and small enterprises being 5.9 and 6 persons respectively. Given cultural traditions in Ethiopia where women are primary household carers, it would seem likely that many of the women interviewed have significant domestic workloads alongside running their own businesses.

2.1.4 Educational Level

A Government survey of Ethiopian women entrepreneurs in the informal sector showed that the majority (59 per cent) of those interviewed were illiterate, with only 20 per cent having received elementary education (CSA, 1997). By contrast, Table 4 shows that 90 per cent of microenterprise owners, and 88 per cent of small enterprise owners report that they had had formal education, with 72 per cent and 66 per cent having received primary and secondary education respectively.

Table 4:   Formal Education by Type of Enterprise

Formal Education	Type of Enterprise		Frequency	%
	Microenterprise (2-5 employees)	Small Enterprise (above 5 employees)		
Yes	61	51	112	91.1
No	7	4	11	8.9
Total	**68**	**55**	**123**	**100.0**

Figure 1 shows that a great number of the women entrepreneurs interviewed had taken some form of professional training. In this respect the women entrepreneurs would appear to have the educational background to manage or at least learn how to manage their businesses.

Figure 1

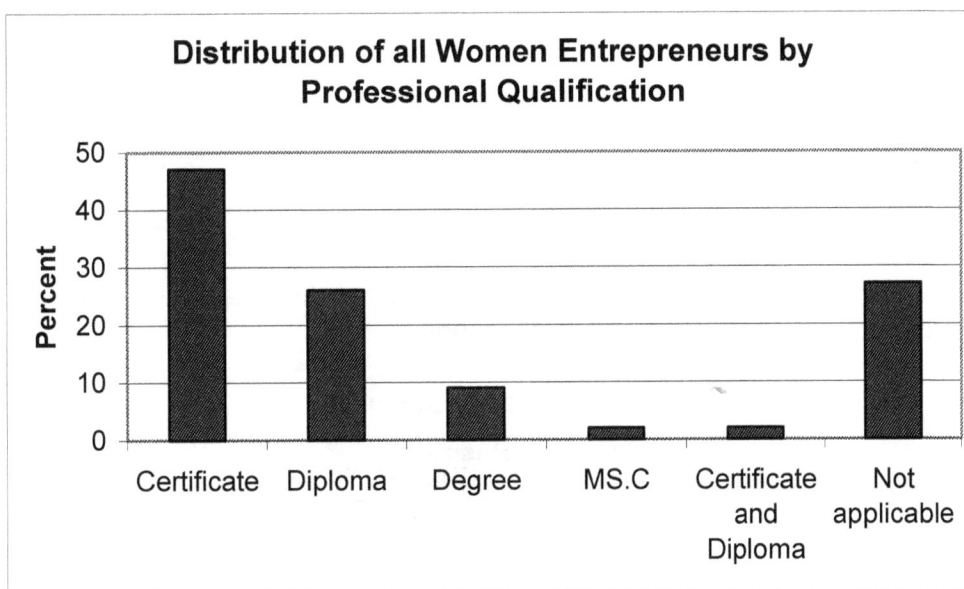

Distribution of all Women Entrepreneurs by Professional Qualification

2.1.5 Previous Job and Work Experience before Starting the Current Business

As Table 5 indicates, nearly half (47 per cent) of the women interviewed were economically active prior to running their current business – either in employment (31 per cent) or working in another business (16 per cent); 20 per cent of the women had been students; 25 per cent had been housewives, and 5 per cent were unemployed before starting their businesses.

Table 5:   Position Prior to Starting their Business

Position	Frequency	%
Employed	38	30.9
Housewife	30	24.8
Student	24	19.5
Another Business	19	15.8
Unemployed	6	4.9
Others	5	4.1
Total	**123**	**100.0**

The women were asked if they felt they had any prior work experience related to their business before starting it. As Table 6 shows nearly a third of those responding said that they had substantial work experience relating to their business prior to start-up. However many (48 per cent) 'just started' with no prior experience at all.

Table 6:   Work Experience Relating to the Current Business

Level of Relevant Experience	Frequency	%
No – just started	59	48.0
Yes – substantial	38	30.9
Very little	26	21.1
Total	**123**	**100.0**

Those with experience had gained it from a number of different sources. Interestingly, over a third of the women had gained experience from running their own businesses, with the majority gaining experience through involvement in a family business (as shown in Table 7).

Table 7:   Source of Previous Experience

Source of Experience	Frequency	%
My family's business	26	40.6
My own business	23	36.0
Other people's business	15	23.4
Total	**64**	**100.0**

The women were asked if these businesses were still operating, and as Table 8 indicates, the majority (72 per cent) were still in operation.

Table 8:   Business Still Operating by the Owner of the Business

Business Still Operating ?	Owner of the Business			
	Other people	Myself	My family	Frequency
Yes	13	8	25	46
No	2	13	1	16
Non Response	-	2	-	2
Total	**15**	**23**	**26**	**64**

Although only 21 of the 23 who previously had own businesses responded, of these 8 have businesses that are still operating, and 25 of the 26 family businesses are still operating.

To summarize, the group of women in the survey are running business at a time in their life when it is normal for them to have substantive family responsibilities, and many of the women come from large households. Having said this, the majority of the women have been formally educated to at least secondary level, they have had some form of employment and / or business experience prior to running their current business, and over a third had previously owned their own business or worked in their family's business.

2.2   A Profile of the Women's Enterprises

As noted earlier the sample of women's businesses was fairly evenly split between micro and small-sized businesses - 68 (or 55 per cent) running microenterprises (with 2-5 employees), and 55 (or 45 per cent) running small enterprises (with more than 5 employees).

2.2.1 Sectors, Products and Services

Table 9 shows that the largest group of women (44 per cent) operated enterprises in the services sector, followed by nearly a third in the trade sector.

Table 9:   Sector of Business (by Enterprise Category)

| Sector in which the Business is | Category of Enterprise | | Frequency | % |
	Micro (2-5 employee)	Small enterprise (above 5)		
Services	23	31	54	43.9
Trade	27	10	37	30.1
Production	7	11	18	14.6
Trade + service	10	3	13	10.6
Handicraft	1	-	1	0.8
Total	**68**	**55**	**123**	**100.0**

Looking at the differences between the micro and small-scale enterprises, it can be seen that a larger percentage of the micro sector are trading businesses (39 per cent as compared to 17 per cent).   This is a very common characteristic of smaller businesses throughout the world.   Trading businesses usually require the least capital and business know-how to start up, and therefore are attractive as "easy entry" and lower risk activities.   The range of products and services produced and supplied by the women's enterprises surveyed is illustrated in Table 10 – no values have been assigned in this table.

Table 10:   Major Products and Services of the Micro and Small Enterprises Surveyed

Category	Microenterprise	Small-scale Enterprise
Services		
	Snacks	Hotels, pensions and restaurants
	Tea& coffee	Education and training
	Hair dressing	Garage services
	Tailoring	Fuel, lubricants and car wash services
	Secretarial services	Laundry services
		Health care services
Trade		
	Sales of souvenirs	Super markets
	Sales of cosmetics	Sales of drugs
	Sales of ready-made clothes	Sales of auto spare parts
	Sales of different products	Sales of computers & computer accessories
	Sales of flower and gift articles	Import and export
Production		
	Handicrafts	Flourmills
		Pastries
		Bakery
		Woodworking
		Production of building materials
		Garments

2.2.2 The Market for Products and Services

As Table 11 shows, the women's businesses were primarily locally based, and almost all of the women interviewed (97.5 per cent of those who responded to this question) stated that they sold most of their products in their local area. All of the microenterprises sold their products locally, with only 3 of the 54 small enterprise respondents selling outside of their local area.

This confirms that women's enterprises tend to rely on potential customers in the immediate vicinity or neighborhood of their enterprises, and may be an indication that women are more restricted in their mobility than male entrepreneurs. The mobility of women entrepreneurs can be restricted due to their multiple responsibilities as homemakers and entrepreneurs, which makes it difficult for them to penetrate into markets that are beyond their local areas.

The types of businesses most women are engaged in are those that can be conveniently operated around their homestead. The survey showed that most of women did not aggressively promote their businesses. Of those who did, 68.5 per cent relied on word of mouth as their primary means of promotion. However, women entrepreneurs who have established businesses in sectors where they can benefit from promotional services are not always encouraged to do so. A good example of this is where the husband of one entrepreneur criticised her for the expense of advertising her business on TV, which affected her confidence and yet was good for business.

Table 11: Scope of Markets

Scope of Market	Frequency	Percentage of Responses
Local market – area of work/residence	117	95.2
Regional markets - capital city of the regional state	1	0.8
National – market	2	1.6
Non-response	3	2.4
Total	**123**	**100.0**

2.2.3 Date of Establishment

The majority of the businesses in the survey (54 per cent) had been established since 1995, a factor which may be associated with the change in Government in 1991 and the subsequent liberalization of the Ethiopian economy. The oldest business had started in 1950 and had been bought as a "going concern" business by the women in the survey. The most recent businesses (7) had been formally operating for just over 6 months, and these had been started either by the women themselves or with their husband or other family members. There is a higher percentage of businesses started by women only (62 per cent) among the micro group of enterprises than among the small enterprises (51per cent), as illustrated in Table 12.

2.2.4 Other Enterprise Characteristics

Table 12:   Who Initiated the Business (by Business Category)

Initiator	Micro	%	Small	%	Both	%
Myself	42	61.8	28	50.9	70	56.9
My Husband	11	16.2	11	20.0	22	17.9
Other Family Members	7	10.3	3	5.5	10	8.1
Took Over Established Business	1	1.5	8	14.5	9	7.3
Friends	3	4.4	3	5.5	6	4.9
Myself and My Husband	2	2.9	1	1.8	3	2.4
Bought Existing Business	-	-	1	1.8	1	0.8
Others	2	2.9	-	-	2	1.6
Total	**68**	**100.0**	**55**	**100.0**	**123**	**100.0**

Table 13:   Form of Ownership (by Enterprise Category)

Form of Ownership	Business Category			%
	Micro	Small	Total	%
Individual – Sole Trader	60	42	102	82.9
Partnership	5	4	9	7.4
Private Ltd	1	6	7	5.7
Share Company	-	2	2	1.6
Other	1	-	1	0.8
Non Response	1	1	2	1.6
Total	**68**	**55**	**123**	**100.0**

As Table 13 indicates, the majority of businesses (both micro and small) were registered as sole trading businesses. Those registered as limited companies tended to be in the "small" category. There was very little relationship between the formality of structure and the age of the business, although the business established in 1950 was one of the two companies with shares.

Table 14:   Working Premises of the Businesses

Ownership of Working Premises	Frequency	%
Rented	73	59.3
Owned	45	36.6
Others	3	2.4
Owned & Rented	1	0.8
Non Response	1	0.8
Total	**123**	**100.0**

When asked about premises, all of the women that responded (122 out of 123) said that they had dedicated premises from which they ran their business. A third of the women owned their premises, but the majority were renting them.

2.2.5 Employment Generated by the Women's Enterprises

The majority of the women entrepreneurs (some 85 per cent of respondents) are engaged full-time in their businesses, that is, their businesses are providing them with full-time employment. In many cases the women's businesses were also generating employment for others.

Table 15: Women Entrepreneurs' Full-time Engagement in Business

	Frequency	%
Yes	104	84.6
No	17	13.8
Non Response	2	1.6
Total	**123**	**100.0**

When asked about the size of their businesses, 120 out of 123 women surveyed were able to give complete details of the numbers they employed. These 120 businesses provided a total of 825 jobs. As Table 16 shows, most of the jobs are full-time paid jobs (72 per cent); 5 per cent of jobs are full-time paid jobs for family members; 14 per cent part-time, and 9 per cent are unpaid or on a "paid in kind" basis.

These figures support the widely held view about the increasing role played by micro- and small enterprises as the generators of jobs. However, they also demonstrate that women entrepreneurs in both micro and small enterprises can generate significant employment opportunities, and thereby contribute to the reduction of poverty in Ethiopia. This challenges the commonly portrayed images of women's businesses as sole traders and informal type of enterprises.

Table 16: Employment in the Enterprises and Sex of Employees (by Enterprise Category)

Type of Employment	Micro		Small		Both		Total	
	Female	Male	Female	Male	Female	Male	Frequency	%
Full-time	99	42	181	270	280	312	592	71.8
Part-time	5	8	40	59	45	67	112	13.6
Paid family members	8	7	14	15	22	22	44	5.3
Unpaid family members	25	13	16	23	41	36	77	9.3
Total	**137**	**70**	**251**	**367**	**388**	**437**	**825**	**100.0**

In terms of the employment profile of the women's enterprises, the survey results show that the average size of enterprises is between 4 and 6.8 persons respectively, depending on whether the median or the mean is taken as the average. The average employment size of women-operated microenterprises is around 3.2 persons, while the average for women-operated small enterprises is 11.2 persons.   Both of these figures are higher than those found in the two CSA surveys conducted on handicraft and manufacturing industries, and the study on the informal sector in all the major towns of the country.   According to these surveys (CSA, 1997), "small enterprises" employ three persons on average.

Table 17 shows the wide range of employment size in the enterprises surveyed, ranging from one business with 46 employees (in various categories of jobs), to four operating with only one additional employee. The most common size of business had two or three employees.   The business with 46 employees produces building materials, has one full-time female and 13 full-time male workers, 31 part-time male workers, and one unpaid family member.

Table 17:   **Number of Employees in the Business**

Number ôf Employees	Frequency	%
1 – 5	69	56.1
6 - 10	25	20.4
11-15	18	14.7
16-20	3	2.4
21-30	4	3.2
47	1	0.8
Non-Response	3	2.4
Total	**123**	**100.0**

To summarize, the survey included a range of enterprises.   Whilst many of these businesses were in what might be termed "traditional female sectors", they were also enterprises based in business premises and employing others – not a typical characteristic attributed to the majority of women's enterprises in Africa.

16

3. Experiences of Starting and Growing a Business

Having looked at the profiles and characteristics of the women entrepreneurs and their businesses, this next section examines the experiences of and issues faced by the women in setting up, managing and growing their businesses.

3.1 The Start-up Experience

A key element of the research was to understand why and how the women had come to actually starting and owning a business.

3.1.1 Motivations for Business Ownership

The women were asked why they had chosen to run their own business as opposed to pursuing another economic option such as seeking employment. Table 18 shows the major reasons given for this choice. The desire to be self-employed was the dominant (45 per cent) reason for women choosing to start a business, followed by business being a family tradition (21.1 per cent).

Table 18: The Primary Reasons Given for Choosing to Start their Own Business

Primary Reasons for business ownership	Frequency	%
To be self-employed	55	44.7
Family Tradition	26	21.1
Brings high income	17	13.8
No other alternative for income	13	10.6
Small investment is required	4	3.3
Others	8	6.5
Total	**123**	**100.0**

When multiple responses were taken into account, a similar profile of preferences appeared with slightly more emphasis on income generation (see Table 19).

Table 19: Reasons Given for Choosing to Start their Own Business – Multiple Choices

Preferences	Frequency	%
To be Self-Employed	59	40.2
Family Tradition	26	17.7
Brings high income	23	15.6
No other alternative is available	22	14.9
Small Investment is required	5	3.4
Other	12	8.2
Total number of responses	**147**	**100.0**

The women were then asked what they felt were the three most critical motivating factors, which helped them to practically pursue business ownership, and whether their family members had been supportive of them in this decision.

On the women entrepreneurs surveyed, 121 out of 123 gave clear statements about what were their critical motivating factors. These statements have been grouped under seven headings, as shown in Tables 20 and 21. In terms of motivation, the women seem to have been particularly motivated by the desire to generate income and support for their families, as well as seeing the business as a vehicle for being independent.

Table 20: Factors Prompting the Start of Businesses

Motivating Factors	Frequency	%
Desire to be self-employed and to become independent	45	36.6
Income generation and to support the family	31	25.2
Had an interest in the line of work and to exploit an opportunity	21	17.1
Had training and entrepreneurial qualification in the business area	11	8.9
Encouragement from family and friends to go into a business	8	6.5
Relatively favorable policy environment	5	4.1
Other	2	1.6
Total	**123**	**100.0**

When the multiple responses were taken into account, the profile of the reasons given was similar as shown in Table 21, with the primary drivers being the desire to be independent and generate income.

Table 21: The Three Most Motivating Factors – Combined Responses

Motivating Factors	Frequency	% of responses
Desire to be self-employed and to become independent	85	31.6
Income generation and to support family	67	24.8
Had an interest in the line of work and to exploit an opportunity	36	13.3
Had training and entrepreneurial qualification in the business area	31	11.5
Encouragement from family and friends to go into a business	24	8.9
Relatively favorable policy environment	9	3.3
Other factors	18	6.6
Total	**270**	**100.0**

3.1.2 Attitudes of the Family at Start-up

Tables 22 and 23 show that the majority of spouses (over 60 per cent) and other family members were very supportive of the women starting a business.

Table 22: Attitudes of Spouse when Starting a Business

Attitude of Spouse	Frequency	%
Very supportive	63	51.2
Supportive	27	22.0
Not supportive	6	5.9
Reacted badly	1	0.8
Non-Responses (no spouse)	26	21.1
Total	**123**	**100.0**

The responses are from women who said they were married, divorced, separated or widowed.

Table 23: Attitudes of other Family Members when Starting Business

Attitudes	Frequency	%
Very supportive	72	58.5
Supportive	34	27.6
Indifferent	3	2.4
Not supportive	6	4.9
Reacted badly	1	0.8
Non-Responses	7	5.7
Total	**123**	**100**

Only one woman reported that her spouse had reacted badly but the rest of the family had supported her, whilst another reported that although her spouse was very supportive her other family members reacted badly. While the family appears to be supportive, the research was interested to see whether this support translated into practical contributions to household chores and childcare. The survey did not probe this in any great detail, but asked the women whether they received such practical help – 54 per cent of the women said they did.

The attitudes of the spouse or other family members when a women tries to be self-employed tend to depend on the type of business activity and the scale of the enterprise, as well as the socio-economic background of the family. If a young woman from a poor family starts a microenterprise to support herself and her family, it is highly unlikely that the family will oppose her efforts to be self-employed – unless the nature of the work is such that it exposes her to situations that may not culturally acceptable to the family. There is the case of the young woman entrepreneur who is running a tailoring school. Although her father supported the idea of her being self-employed, he opposed to the idea of her moving out of her parents' house to be near her business. Women who start small enterprises directly themselves because they have the necessary resources, sometimes face opposition from their husbands or other family members, especially if the type of activity is traditionally not thought to be a "respectable" business for women. For example, one woman who now runs a printing business was in the hotel business beforehand and faced some criticism. Likewise, the woman entrepreneur who has a bakery business faced opposition from her husband when she wanted to start a typing school. She later divorced, and felt this was mainly because she restricted to stay at home.

3.1.3 Constraints at Start-up

Most new business starts-ups, no matter how simple or complex, face some challenges in during the process of starting up. When asked about such challenges, the women entrepreneurs stated a number of problems they had encountered during the start-up phase (see Table 24).

Table 24: Major Constraints Faced During Establishment

Constraints	Frequency	%
Working space	51	41.5
Lack of credit facility	41	33.3
Lack of appropriately skilled labour	8	6.5
Government rules and regulations	4	3.2
Lack of support service that would build confidence	3	2.4
Obtaining licences	3	2.4
Access to raw materials	1	0.8
Others	5	4.1
No Response	7	5.7
Total	**123**	**100.0**

The two most notable constraints were lack of appropriate working space (the problem mentioned most frequently by 44 per cent of respondents), followed by lack of credit facilities (35 per cent).

Clearly many of the women entrepreneurs have tried to overcome some if not all of their problems, in so far as they have actually established their businesses. The important additional question is, "Would these businesses continue operating or develop further?" The women were asked how they had overcome their problems and constraints, and the following are the most commonly mentioned actions.

Space issues
- Paying exorbitant rentals in the absence of own premises
- Managed to work in confined premises
- Adapted to limited resources
- Used small working premises

Finance issues
- Loans from moneylenders
- Loans from banks
- Credit in kind
- Devised ways to make credit suppliers trust me
- Rented machinery
- Using traditional revolving fund system (equb)
- Used parents' house as collateral
- Leased my house

Labour issues
- Increased wages
- Replaced unskilled labour with skilled labour
- Trained employees

General
- Support and assistance from relatives and spouses
- Through patience and persistence
- Lessons learned from mistakes
- Networking

The research showed that the women used various means to overcome some of the problems they faced during the start-up phase. For instance, they tried to mitigate problems by finding short-term temporary solutions, like borrowing money from local moneylenders, accessing credit in kind etc. Nonetheless, the terms and conditions of both these sources of credit tend to be exploitative and therefore puts the sustainability of these young enterprises at stake. Such temporary solutions do not pave the way for the eventual growth and development of the enterprises. In fact, this could be one of the reasons why many of the registered enterprises close down in their early years. It was surprising to find out during the survey that a number of women registered as operating enterprises and on the list of the regional bureaux had in fact ceased trading.

The same is true of the solutions that the women entrepreneurs applied to overcoming the problem of finding premises for production and sales. Many indicated that they were renting premises for their enterprises but paying very high rent. Some of them were operating from home, regardless of the market access problems that this brought. In one of the case studies, it is pointed out that one woman sometimes asks herself if she would have the guts to continue running her existing business for the next five years under the current unfavorable support environment. "I can't answer that question", she said.

3.1.4 Start-up Funding

(i)   Capital invested in Start-up:

Table 25 indicates that the women entrepreneurs required a wide range of differing levels of capital to establish their businesses.   Some were as low as Birr 40 (approximately USD 5*) and others as high as Birr 700,000 (USD 82,352). Most (75 per cent) of the women entrepreneurs running micro businesses stated that they had required less than Birr 10,000 (USD 1,176) to set up their businesses, whereas about 10 per cent of them had invested over Birr 20,000 (USD 2,353) to start their activities. Similarly, 75 per cent of the women entrepreneurs engaged in small-scale businesses required about Birr 34,000 (USD 4,000) to establish their enterprises, whereas a smaller number (about 10 per cent) had invested over Birr 78,000 (USD 9,176) to set up their businesses.

Table 25:   Costs of Establishing the Business

Cost to set up Business (Birr)	Micro	Small	Total	%
<1000	5	2	7	5.6
>1000 – 5000	28	8	36	29.4
>5000 – 10,000	21	4	25	20.3
>10,000 – 20,000	8	5	13	10.6
>20,000 – 50,000	2	15	17	13.8
>50,000 – 100,000	2	8	10	8.1
>100,000	-	8	8	6.5
Non-Response	2	5	7	5.7
Total	**68**	**55**	**123**	**100.0**

* The exchange rate was 8.6 Birr to 1 USD at the time of the study.

Looking at the relative amounts of investment in the different sectors within the survey, it is evident that higher capital outlays were required in the production and service sectors i.e., an average of Birr 42,000 (USD4.941) and Birr 45,000(USD 5,294) respectively, compared to Birr 17,700 (USD 2,082) in the trade sector. This is because production and service sector activities usually require more machinery, equipment, tools, materials and facilities, which imply larger investment outlays compared to trading activities.

(ii)   Sources of Start-up Capital

The main sources of start-up capital for women entrepreneurs in the survey included personal savings (53 per cent), followed by household finance (16 per cent), and assistance from friends and relatives (10 per cent), as shown in Table 26. Only four per cent of the women entrepreneurs surveyed obtained bank loans to start their businesses.

Table 26: Main Source of Start-up Funding (by Enterprise Category)

Main Source of Start-up Funding	Microenterprise	Small enterprise	Total	%
Personal Saving	33	31	64	52.0
Household	14	5	19	15.4
Assistance from friends/relatives	7	5	12	9.8
Borrowed from relatives or friends/money lenders	6	4	10	8.1
Equb*	3	4	7	5.7
Borrowed from Bank	3	2	5	4.1
Inheritance	-	2	2	1.6
Assistance from NGOs	1	-	1	0.8
Micro Finance	1	-	1	0.8
Others	-	2	2	1.6
Total	**68**	**55**	**123**	**100.0**

* Equb is the name for informal group savings/lending schemes in Ethiopia.

When one considers the situation on the basis of the categories of micro and small enterprises, the same pattern appears to apply with only a slight difference in the percentages. Personal savings account for 49 per cent and 57 per cent of women entrepreneurs' sources of start up capital for those engaged in micro and small enterprises, respectively. The second and third largest sources of start-up capital appear to be household finances (21 per cent for micro and 9 per cent for small enterprises), and assistance from relatives and friends (10 per cent for micro and 9 per cent for small enterprise operators).

Of those women entrepreneurs who had access to bank loans for start-up capital, 5 per cent are micro and 4 per cent small enterprises. The bank loans for women entrepreneurs starting up microenterprises came from both formal banks and Micro Finance Institutions (MFIs), while those women who established small-scale enterprises obtained credit from formal commercial banks only. This latter group of women entrepreneurs reported that they did not consider MFIs relevant for their purposes, which is likely to be due to the smaller loan sizes offered by the MFIs. This is also corroborated by the findings pf several reports reviewed in the secondary research phase, showing that women entrepreneurs running small-scale enterprises were not keen to get loans from MFIs due to their low loan ceiling.

3.1.4 Working Premises

As noted earlier, the majority of women entrepreneurs do not own their own working premises. A large proportion of women enterprises (60 per cent) carry out their activities in rented premises by paying very high rent. The distribution of women's enterprises by ownership of premises is shown in Table 27.

Table 27: Distribution by Ownership of Premises

Ownership	Frequency			% of Responses
	Micro	Small	Both	
Owned	17	28	45	36.9
Rented	48	25	73	59.8
Owned and Rented	-	1	1	0.8
Others – shared	2	1	3	2.5
Total	**67**	**55**	**122**	**100.0**

A further examination reveals that most women in microenterprises (72 per cent) operate from rented premises, while women in small enterprises operating from rented premises account for about 46 per cent. Although the women reported that they are trying to find temporary solutions to the problem of working space, the issue of lack of permanent solutions remains a constraint to many (44.8 per cent) at start-up and as a factor inhibiting further growth. Issues such as rental levels, terms of the lease, physical conditions and location all likely contribute to a range of premises-related constraints.

As stated earlier, lack of appropriate premises can retard the growth of the enterprise as is illustrated by the case of Mekedes with her handcraft business, and Beldinesh with her tailoring school.

3.1.5 Access to Equipment and Materials during Start-up

The majority of the women entrepreneurs interviewed (70 per cent) brought a wide range of equipment, fittings and materials into their business at the start-up stage. When asked how they set about obtaining equipment for their businesses, 67 per cent of the women who responded obtained their equipment and assets through direct purchases (see Table 28).

Table 28: Ways in which Start-up Assets were Obtained – Primary Means

	Frequency	% of 123	% of Respondents
Purchased	66	53.6	67
Inherited	12	9.8	12.2
Granted	5	4.1	5.1
Leased/granted	4	3.3	4.1
Leased	1	0.8	1.0
Others	10	8.1	10.2
Non-Response	25	20.3	N.A.
Total	**123**	**100.0**	**100.0**

Micro and small enterprises use a variety of means to acquire assets with only a few using leasing. The majority of microenterprises (74.1 per cent) purchased their assets and did not use leasing.

Table 29: The Ways in which Start-up Equipment and Assets were Obtained by Business Category (percentage responses)

Method	Micro- Enterprises	Small Enterprises	All Enterprises
Purchase	74.1	59.1	67.3
Inheritance	7.4	18.2	12.2
Grants	9.3	2.3	5.1
Lease	1.9	6.8	4.1
Others	7.4	13.6	10.2
Total	**100.0**	**100.0**	**100.0**

The category showing equipment and assets obtained through inheritance was much more significant for small enterprises that for the microenterprises.

3.1.7 Support Services Obtained

As there are many challenges and constraints faced at start-up, business support services are often crucial to ensure a relatively smooth passage through this stage of business development. The majority of the women had received no assistance from external support services in establishing their businesses. Of those that did (just under a third of all the women interviewed), most had received support with financial issues, followed by managerial problems and technical problems (see Table 31). In terms of accessing support, the largest group (30 per cent) had done so through friends and family, nearly a quarter through business associations (23.5 per cent), with the others gaining access through a range of banks (1 per cent) and other personal contacts.

Table 30: Receipt of External Formal Support Services

External formal support service received?	Type of Enterprise		Total	
	Micro (2-5 employees)	Small enterprise (above 5)	Frequency	%
Yes	18	16	34	27.6
No	48	37	85	69.2
Non-response	2	2	4	3.2
Total	**68**	**55**	**123**	**100.0**

Table 31: Type of External Formal Support Service Obtained

Type of Support Received	Frequency	% of respondents
Financial	21	61.7
Technical	11	32.3
Managerial	7	20.5
Market Information	4	11.8
Networking	4	11.8
Others	6	17.6
Total respondents	**34**	**100.0**

When the women entrepreneurs were asked about their major forms of support in getting their business started, these were very much in terms of family and friends, as well as in relation to the general environment for business in Ethiopia. Over one-third (39 per cent) of the women entrepreneurs surveyed stated that financial and material support from relatives and friends was their primary support; 14 per cent stated easy access to credit (formally and informally) ; and 11 per cent felt a conducive government policy environment (i.e. the free market economic policy, the right to get organized, etc.) helped them. However, 36 per cent felt they had not got any particular support in starting their business.

If one considers the situation of support at start-up based on the scale of business category, one can observe a broadly similar pattern between the micro and small enterprise owners. For example, 19 per cent and 15 per cent of micro and small enterprise owners respectively had obtained financial support from relatives/friends. One major difference was in the way that they had obtained material support from relatives and friends at start-up – 24 per cent of micro and 8 per cent small enterprises respectively. A likely explanation for this could be that more of the micro operators used materials and equipment for home-based activities whereas many of the small-scale enterprise activities, were setting up their businesses outside of the home.

3.1.8 Attitudes of Women Entrepreneurs towards Self-Employment and their Current Business

As discussed elsewhere in this report, the drive for self-employment is one of the most important factors that motivated women micro and small enterprise operators to establish their own businesses. This fact is supported by the survey findings, as 88 per cent of the operators said they are proud of being self-employed. Furthermore, 75 per cent of women operating both micro and small enterprises stated that even if they were offered permanent job opportunities elsewhere, they would not forego their current businesses.

Table 32: Attitudes towards Self-employment and Alternative Employment

Category of Enterprise	Proud of being Self-employed		Will not leave current business if offered permanent job elsewhere	
	Frequency	% all	Frequency	%
Micro	58	47.2	47	38.2
Small	49	39.9	45	36.6
Indifferent	1	0.8	-	-
Not proud or not leave for a job	15	12.1	31	25.2
Total	**123**	**100**	**123**	**100**

Those who would not forego running their current businesses for permanent jobs elsewhere gave the following reasons for their choice:
- Pride in self-employment;
- Confidence and satisfaction in the business being operated;
- Lack of other skills;
- To keep the family tradition.

Women engaged in microenterprise activities who would leave their business if offered permanent jobs elsewhere, stated the following reasons for their decisions:-
- To get better paying jobs;
- To get an opportunity to improve and pursue education/study;
- Leave business to the family and engage oneself in a better opportunity;
- Permanent job is an easier way to earn a living;
- Current business performance is not satisfactory.

3.2   Managing the Business

Having examined the experiences and issues faced in establishing their businesses, the survey went on to explore the women's experiences in managing and further developing their businesses. This looked at decision-making, time in the business, financial management, marketing and the formalizing of the business.

At the outset of this discussion it is important to note that at start-up most of the women entrepreneurs stated that they did not get any kind of formal external support (69 per cent of respondents). This would suggest that women entrepreneurs' own strengths and resourcefulness, as well as the support obtained from close relatives and friends, played a major role in the establishment and running of their new enterprises.

3.2.1 Decision-making

The survey findings showed that women entrepreneurs are largely independent in making decisions concerning their businesses, particularly with regard to the utilization of the money generated from their businesses, 76 per cent of micro-entrepreneurs and 83 per cent of small-scale entrepreneurs make decisions with regard to the utilization of money generated from their businesses. Other women entrepreneurs also make some major decisions that affect the activities of the businesses by their own, such as taking bank loans and transferring ownership (69 per cent in microenterprises and 61 per cent in small-scale enterprises). There is also a significant involvement of husbands/spouses in making joint decisions – 32 per cent in the case of small-scale enterprises, and 18 per cent in microenterprises.

This confirms the fact that as women start generating their own income they are more empowered to make their own decisions. It can be argued that their economic empowerment is a basis for social empowerment as well. The survey reveals that about 32 per cent of the women engaged in small enterprises make joint decisions with their spouses. This could indicate a number of things: for example, to run a small enterprise the resources required are relatively higher than for microenterprises, and it can also entail the purchase of machinery and other fixed assets. The management can also be more complex, and this may lead some women entrepreneurs to seek the assistance of the spouse or other family members. If the woman wants to borrow from a bank by offering some sort of fixed asset as collateral, such as a house, she will need the consent of the husband because in Ethiopia title deeds to a house are usually in the name of both spouses. Therefore, it requires a joint decision to be able to offer it as collateral or to use it as premises for the business.

Although most of the women said they make decisions about their businesses on their own, some of them reported that they do it on a trial and error basis because they didn't have prior managerial and technical training or adequate education to manage the business effectively. Decisions regarding sophisticated managerial, financial and technical issues appear to be difficult for some of the women entrepreneurs. The case study of Romana and her printing business is a good illustration. She decided to buy a printing machine accessory without consulting anyone, and later found out that it was not compatible with her existing machine. This was a costly mistake. On the other hand Semret, who is a relatively well-educated woman entrepreneur, decided to hire an expert for a short period because she didn't have the specific skills necessary for the bakery business.

A significant number of women entrepreneurs who are engaged in growth-oriented and small enterprises are making use of the support, skills and assistance of their spouses. In some cases, this is not surprising as the spouses were involved with developing the business in the first instance.

When the women entrepreneurs were asked if they found making business decisions difficult, the majority (54 per cent being 53 of the 92 who responded) said not. Of the 39 who said that they had problems, many (33 per cent) concerned financial matters (borrowing money and tax issues) and marketing/selling (28 per cent) issues (pricing, shifting location, diversification).

3.2.2 Time Spent in and Rewards from the Business

Tables 15 (above) and Table 33 (below) show that 85 per cent of women entrepreneurs are fully engaged in running their businesses. The full-time engagement does not show any significant variation between micro and small enterprise operators.

Table 33: Full-time Engagement and Payment of Salary (by Enterprise Category)

Category of Enterprise	Full-time Engagement		Pay themselves Wages/Salaries	
	Frequency	%	Frequency	%
Micro	58	84	11	16
Small	46	85	20	36
Total	**104**	**85**	**36**	**30**

However, less than one-third (30 per cent) of the surveyed women enterprise operators indicated that they pay themselves wages/salaries on a regular basis. Therefore, many women are working full-time in their businesses and are not receiving a regular income for their efforts. This could be because the women choose not to take a regular salary (only taking income as and when they need it) because they reinvest the money in their business, or because there are insufficient funds in the business to permit a regular wage to be taken. It was also observed that more women small enterprise operators (36 per cent) pay themselves wages on regular basis, as compared to those operating microenterprises (16 per cent).

When the women entrepreneurs who do not pay themselves wages/salaries on regular basis were asked why, the major reasons included:
- There was no need for a regular payment as they could draw the money at any time as they needed;
- They consider profit as their regular wage;
- They do not make adequate profit;
- They were reinvesting their profits;
- The income generated is too low.

As Table 34 shows, the average salary of those paying wages for themselves is Birr 850 per month (USD 100) for both the micro and small enterprise owners. Taking the women entrepreneurs as a whole, 10 per cent of them earn less than Birr 200 on a regular basis, whilst 10 per cent earn more than Birr 2,000 on a regular basis. It is also observed that the average wage for small business enterprise owners (Birr 972) is larger than for microenterprise operators (Birr 575). The average earnings are comparable to a monthly salary paid by public institutions, e.g. a fresh university graduate.

Table 34: Average Regular Wages/Salaries (in Birr) in Women-operated Enterprises

Type of Enterprise	Minimum Salary	Maximum Salary	Average Salary
Micro	100	1,500	575
Small	300	2,500	972
Both	100	2,500	850

These findings provide some insights into how the women manage the money in their business. The women were also asked some direct questions in this respect.

3.2.3 Financial Management

As shown in Table 35, over 50 per cent of both micro and small enterprises keep the money generated from the enterprise separate from their personal money. Women in small enterprises appear to be in a slightly better position in this regard compared to microenterprise operators.

Over half of all the women who responded said that they keep records on costs in order to calculate their profits, however there was a notable difference between micro and small business owners. Women with small enterprises are much better in keeping cost records than microenterprises, although as was noted earlier there is not a significant difference in educational, skill and experience levels between the women entrepreneurs in micro and small enterprises. It may be that the women engaged in small-scale enterprises have had to become more aware and experienced in issues such as record keeping, due to the larger scale of their businesses and greater exposure to formal licensing and tax requirements, than those women engaged in microenterprises.

Table 35: Management of Money and Record-keeping (by Enterprise Category)

Type of Enterprises	Keep Enterprises' Money Separate		Keep Record on Cost	
	Frequency	%	Frequency	%
Micro	34	50	33	49
Small	30	54	33	60

3.2.4 Marketing and Promotional Activities

As noted earlier, local markets (i.e. those in the immediate area of work/ residence make up the main markets (95 per cent) for the products/services of the women entrepreneurs in the survey. This is particularly true for those women engaged in microenterprise activities. Only very few small-scale business operators indicated that they supply their goods/services to the main regional markets. This would appear to suggest that the women entrepreneurs have limited experience of marketing and selling to distant markets, where they may be able to find better price advantages.

Essentially, most of the women entrepreneurs would appear to be facing stiff competition with others for a limited clientele in small local markets, and they are not actively seeking (or knowing about) potential opportunities for getting better prices for their products and services further afield. The survey results also showed that 59 per cent of the women entrepreneurs do not use any promotional means to advertise their businesses. The major promotional technique used by many (69 per cent) is by word of mouth and through the use of signboards, both of which tend to be locally focused.

When asked about their sales and marketing channels, 86 per cent of the women entrepreneurs said that they relied on themselves to market and promote their products and services directly. About 10 per cent indicated that their production and market depended solely on orders from clients, and a further 3 per cent said that they sold to and through retailers. This profile of marketing practices and experiences would suggest that many of the women entrepreneurs do not have good networks, and limited contact with wholesalers or trading houses who could be used to market their products further afield. This challenge is linked with the problem of inadequate infrastructure (roads, transport, communications, etc.) to neighbouring markets, which makes it difficult for the women entrepreneurs to go there themselves.

When the women were asked about their main marketing constraints, some of the major issues identified were as follows:

- Lack of suitable location or sales outlet
- Stiff competition
- Low purchasing power of the local population

- Lack of marketing know how
- Seasonal nature of the business
- Lack of market information
- Inadequate infrastructure
- Shortage of time (due to multiple tasks)
- Shortage of raw materials
- Shortage of working capital

Women entrepreneurs in both micro and small enterprise repeatedly referred to these largely marketing-based constraints. This implies that regardless of the scale of the enterprises, most women entrepreneurs seem to have common marketing problems. Further details from the survey would indicate that many of these problems emanate from their limited mobility and multiple responsibilities as homemakers and entrepreneurs. They cannot aggressively penetrate into market niches beyond their areas of operation because of the above reasons, and also this is compounded by their lack of marketing know how. They are often unable to afford to have market research conducted in their areas of business due to limited resources. Cultural and social class issues also impinge upon their entrepreneurial behaviour, such that they may shy away from processes that involve "aggressive" sales and marketing activities. The case of the women in the printing business is a good example. She said that to compensate for her weakness in marketing, she had to employ a salesman, even though her enterprise is a small-scale business that ought to have been able to cope without engaging a specialized "salesman".

3.2.5 Formalizing the Business

All of the businesses surveyed in this research were registered – or at least listed as registered businesses. When the women were asked whether they were aware of government regulations affecting their businesses, 72 per cent said that they were, with a slightly higher percentage of the positive responses from the small business category (80 per cent), than the microenterprises (67 per cent). Those who said they were aware of regulations were then asked, "Have you tried to comply with those regulations?" Some 86 per cent responded positively, although their attempts had not been without problems. Nearly 20 per cent of those responding had had no problems with the registration process, and for the rest the main complaints were about the level of taxes (43 per cent), cumbersome bureaucracy to get services (9 per cent), unfair/unrealistic service charges (5 per cent), and a general lack of information about how to obtain licences, such as procedures and location of offices (6 per cent). Five of the women micro-entrepreneurs who responded to these questions had been involved in litigation over registration matters.

During the survey some of the women engaged in microenterprises expressed the opinion that they prefer to remain unlicensed, although they have been registered with some of the authorities. They indicated that they are afraid that they may not be able to comply with the regulations – especially the high level of taxes – if they are licensed. Being "registered" and "licensed" are two different things. Enterprises are registered to show that they have a legal entity (to sue and be sued). However, some microenterprises start up and can be closed down easily (or temporarily) if necessary. In some cases for instance, where the women is a nursing mother and she does not have any one to assist her in the business, she may have to close it down temporarily.

In the survey, there was a question about whether the women have temporarily closed down their businesses during the last two years. Just four of the women indicated that their enterprises had been closed down temporarily for reasons known to themselves. At times, family responsibilities oblige them to close down or transfer the business to others. The woman in the printing business is a case in point: while she was running her small hotel, she temporarily leased it to someone on contract basis because she had to attend to her children who were going to school abroad. Having reflected on some of the general management issues involved in running their businesses, the women entrepreneurs were asked more specifically about their views and experiences in trying to grow and further develop their businesses beyond start-up.

3.3   Growing the Business

The survey showed that about 70 per cent of the women entrepreneurs who are currently engaged in small-scale undertakings had started as microenterprise operators and grew to small-scale operators, which means that within the sample there has been some significant experience of growing a business. The women were asked a range of questions to reflect on their past business performance, issues of success, and plans for the future of their businesses.

3.3.1 Attitudes to Growth
Firstly, the women entrepreneurs were asked how they considered and measured growth in their business. Their responses show that a number of yardsticks are used to measure growth, and the following are the most common measurement criteria mentioned by respondents (n = 110):
- Increase in enterprise income (19)
- Increase in number of customers (16)
- Increase in number of products/services (diversification) (9)
- Expand market (7)
- Increase in number of employees (5)
- Increase in stock (4)
- Meet personal and family needs (4)
- Expansion of activities (2)
- Increase in capital and fixed assets (2)
- Improvement in living conditions (2).

3.3.2 Attitudes to Success

As far as success in business is concerned, Table 36 reveals that 73 per cent of the women entrepreneurs feel that they are "successful" in their businesses. It is observed that more women operating small enterprises feel they are successful (85 per cent) than those women operating microenterprises (63 per cent).

Table 36: Distribution of Women Entrepreneurs Reporting Success (per cent)

Type of Enterprise	Successful		Not Successful	
	Frequency	%	Frequency	%
Micro	42	63	25	37
Small	45	85	8	15
All	**87**	**72**	**33**	**27**

The "successful" women entrepreneurs (84) defined success in their business in a number of different ways as illustrated below:

- Profitability of the business (20)
- Business enables support to family (14)
- Self esteem/satisfaction in the business (11)
- Income is growing (7)
- Business is expanding (5)
- Increased number of customers (4)
- Supplying more goods (4)
- Business is running smoothly (2)
- Opportunity for self-employment (created job for myself) (2)

Those who felt that they were not successful mentioned the following as criteria for their indicators for lack of success:

- Lack of market (9)
- Business is not profitable (6)
- Lack of adequate funds (3)
- Lack of skill and marketing know – how (3)
- Not personally satisfying work (3)
- Lack of suitable location (2)

3.3.3 Expansion and Diversification of the Women's Enterprises

According to the survey, 67 per cent of women entrepreneurs have expanded or diversified their businesses in terms of the range of products and services since establishment. A greater proportion (76 per cent) of women in growth-oriented small-scale enterprises undertook expansion or diversification compared to those with microenterprises (60 per cent). The difference in the degree of expansion or diversification between the micro and small enterprises is attributed mainly to the difference in opportunities for expansion that are available for women entrepreneurs engaged in micro and small business activities.

Table 37 shows the main ways in which the women entrepreneurs described the development of their businesses. These included expanding the size of enterprise (34 per cent), addition of new products (26 per cent), and hiring more workers (21 per cent), which were the most important ones. Some women (10 per cent) indicated that they have improved the quality of their products as a measure of expansion and development, whereas less than 10 per cent of the women entrepreneurs stated that they changed the type of business or started selling in new markets. In addition, 5 per cent of women entrepreneurs rationalized their business by reducing the type of products or the number of employees, and reducing their related costs by buying inputs in bulk to reduce cost and increase efficiency. This situation poses challenges and opportunities for increasing the number of growth-oriented women entrepreneurs, as well as hiring more workers and increasing the range of products and services.

Table 37: Ways of Business Expansion and Diversification

Ways of expansion	Percentage
Expanded size of Enterprise	34
Hired more workers	21
Improved quality of the product	10
Started selling in new markets	7
Ways of Business Diversification	
Added new products	26
Relocated working premises	1
Changed the type of business	1
Rationalization of Business	
Reduced costs by buying inputs in bulk	1
Reduced type of products	1
Reduced number of employees	1
Others	2
Total number of respondents who had expanded/diversified	**82**

The women were then asked how they had acquired the skills and knowledge they needed to develop and grow their businesses. Table 38 (below) shows that previous experience and training played major roles for the expansion and diversification of women-owned enterprises, for both the micro and small enterprise categories. A greater proportion of microenterprise owners than small-scale owners appeared to rely on their own experience, which a greater proportion of small enterprise owners used training as a source of know-how. Support from business advisory services was considered as a source of ideas for the expansion and diversification of businesses by 5 per cent of respondents.

Table 38: Sources of 'Know-how' Acquired for Diversification/Expansion

Sources of skill	Micro	Small
Own Previous Experience	69	58
Training	14	31
Advice from others	5	4
Other sources	7	4
Non-response	5	2
Total	**100.0**	**100.0**

3.3.4 Obstacles to Growth

Women entrepreneurs were asked: "What are the three biggest obstacles you face in developing your business?" As Tables 39 and 40 show, there is a wide range of factors which the women feel inhibit their business development. Taking the greatest obstacle first, Table 39 shows that a lack of capital, a general lack of confidence to take greater risks, and lack of skills in negotiation are seen as the biggest barriers to women in growing their businesses. These applied to both those running microenterprises and small enterprises.

Table 39: The Biggest Obstacles Faced in Developing Business

Obstacles	Frequency	%
Lack of adequate working capital	55	48.2
Lack of confidence to take risks in business	25	21.4
Lack of skills in negotiation	11	9.8
Lack of managerial skills	4	3.6
Problems of working space and sales outlet	10	8.9
Others	9	8.0
Total	**114**	**100.0**

When the multiple responses to the three biggest obstacles were considered, the majority of the 114 respondents had only two obstacles, and the balance of barriers changed slightly. Once again, the lack of working capital was seen as the main barrier (30.5 per cent), followed by the lack of managerial skills (15 per cent), and space to expand for production and sales (15 per cent). Also, all three of these factors were seen a slightly more important hurdles by microenterprises as compared to small business – as regards lack of space 66 per cent of those mentioning space problems were microenterprises. This table also shows some of the gender-based problems facing the women entrepreneurs, such as problems of mobility (3.7 per cent) and lack of support from household.

Table 40: Three Biggest Obstacles Faced in Developing Business

Obstacles	Frequency	%
Lack of adequate working capital	74	30.5
Lack of managerial skills	38	15.6
Problems of working space and sales outlet	38	15.6
Lack of confidence to take risks in business	31	12.7
Lack of negotiation skills	11	4.5
Problem of mobility as a result of household chores	9	3.7
Lack of support from the rest of the household members	2	0.8
Others	40	17.3
Total	**243**	**100**

The women entrepreneurs were asked how they cope and try to overcome and tackle these problems. Of those women entrepreneurs responding to this (109), the greatest number (35 per cent) had not yet found solutions. Some of the major strategies mapped out and adopted by the women entrepreneurs to overcome the problems faced while trying to develop their enterprises included the following:

- Borrowing money from the informal sector
- Using credit from suppliers
- Paying high rentals in the absence of own premises
- Assistance from relatives
- Ploughing back the profit
- Mobilizing Equb
- Seeking advice from other people
- Hiring professional people
- Diversified the products
- Changed location

These solutions do not seem to be much different than those that the women entrepreneurs applied when establishing their enterprises or at the start-up stage. These included borrowing money from the informal sector, seeking assistance from relatives, and paying high house rent. These reveal that the role of the support environment, both financial and non-financial support, in facilitating or hindering women-owned businesses has not changed much over time. However, the women seem to make different sort of efforts to succeed and keep their enterprises going. For example, they ploughed back the profits generated from the business, tried to diversify products, and changed location to overcome the problem of market. They also tried to improve their customer handling and other management skills based on lessons learnt through trial and error.

3.3.5 Current Sources of Business Finance

Lack of working capital was clearly stated as a major barrier to growth by many of the women entrepreneurs, so it was interesting to hear how the women actually funded their businesses. When asked this question directly, many of the women stated that the major source of finance for their businesses came from the proceeds of the businesses which are ploughed back for expansion of the enterprise (68.6 per cent), followed by a long way by loans (18.9 per cent) from banks – more so for small businesses – and MFIs. Table 41 shows other sources which were mainly relatives and friends as interest free loans or grants. Table 42 shows multiple responses to this question, indicating a similar spread of sources as for the single responses. In this case, the microenterprises are slightly more likely to be using MFIs and informal means such as Equbs, than the small business owners.

Table 41: Primary Source of Business Finance (by Business Category)

Current Source of Business Finance	Enterprise Category		Total	
	Micro-Enterprise	Small Enterprise	Frequency	% of Respondents
Ploughed back the profit	51	32	83	68.6
Bank loan	5	12	17	14.1
Credit from micro finance institutions	5	2	7	5.8
Money lenders	3	2	5	4.1
Credit in kind	1	2	3	2.5
Equb*	2	-	2	1.6
Others	-	4	4	3.3
Total numbers responding	**67**	**54**	**121**	**100.0**

* name for the traditional saving mobilization groups in Ethiopia.

Table 42: Multiple Responses to Sources of Business Finance

Current Source of Business Finance	Type of Enterprise		Total	
	Micro (2-5 employees)	Small enterprise (above 5)	Frequency	% of Respondents
Ploughing back the profit	59	42	101	83.5
Bank loan	5	13	18	14.9
Credit from micro finance institutions	5	2	7	5.8
Credit in kind	4	3	7	5.8
Money lenders	3	2	5	4.1
Equb	3	-	3	2.4
Others	10	8	18	14.9
Total numbers responding	**67**	**54**	**121**	

Most of the women running small enterprises cannot access bank credit because of the lack of fixed assets to offer as collateral. Out of the enterprises interviewed, only 13 per cent were able to get a bank loan as they were able to use theirs or their parents' fixed assets as loan security. Even those who have accessed credit complained that the terms and conditions of the loans were not favourable for the type of their enterprises. Some of the examples given were that the repayment schedules set by the banks are not based on the paying capacity of the enterprises, thereby making it very difficult to meet their obligation to the banks, and others mentioned that the loan process was lengthy and tedious. There are no appropriate sources of credit designed for the majority of small enterprises and the growth-oriented microenterprises who need working capital loans that are higher than the loan ceilings of the MFIs. Furthermore, the credit delivery modalities of existing MFIs (mainly group-based) do not fit into the demands of the growth-oriented women entrepreneurs and their enterprises, which require a different range of loan products, such as slightly higher loan amounts, individual loans, and longer repayment periods.

Although the loan ceiling of the MFIs (Birr 5,000) has been increased by the regulatory body, the MFIs themselves do not seem to aggressively implement this because their sources of finance are mainly donors and donors prefer that the fund be channelled to the bottom layers of the microenterprises, and not to the growth-oriented or "small" businesses. Therefore, there is an obvious "missing link" or gap in the provision of credit to most small enterprises and to growth-oriented microenterprises.

The survey reveals that women entrepreneurs in micro and small enterprises have tried to use significant portions of their profits for expanding their enterprises, and others have been borrowing from the informal sector. Borrowing from the informal sector is only a short-term solution because such loans cannot finance the sort of long-term investments that are required to develop and grow their enterprises. This situation will tend to constrain the women's abilities to grow their businesses. Business strategies of expansion, diversification and maintaining market share all require sources of funds, and yet the women entrepreneurs are having to rely primarily on their own resources and the profits from their enterprises. Clearly this situation provides both an opportunity and a challenge for support agencies to be able to offer suitable loan products to women engaged in both micro and small enterprise undertakings.

3.3.6 Problems Affecting the Negotiating Power of Women Entrepreneurs

Negotiation skills are one dimension for women engaged in promoting their businesses, and this appears to be a particular problem for many of the women entrepreneurs. During the survey, some of the women pointed out that due to their upbringing or their background (coming from conservative families), their level of education and lack of exposure, they seem to have problems in situations that require aggressive negotiation or having meetings outside of normal business hours. The case study of the woman involved in the printing business is a good example. She stated that men dominate the printing business and it has been hard for her to win some contracts because it is difficult for her to approach customers on a more informal basis outside office hours, thereby hampering her efforts at building business relationships and networks.

3.3.7 Future Plans and Visions of the Women Entrepreneurs

Having looked at the past and current growth and development of the women's businesses, the research then attempted to evaluate the women's capacities and intentions in relation to planning the future of their business. Accordingly, the women were asked if they had thought about the future at all, and whether they had specific plans for the future of their businesses.

(i) Future Plans

Table 43 shows that about 96 per cent of the women entrepreneurs stated that they had future plans for their businesses – both for the micro and small enterprise categories.

Table 43: Future Plans for the Business

Type of Enterprises	Have Future Plans		Do Not Have Future Plan	
	Frequency	%	Frequency	%
Micro	64	52.0	4	3.2
Small	54	44.0	1	0.8
Both	**118**	**96.0**	**5**	**4.0**

Those women entrepreneurs with future plans indicated the following major components or activities in their plans:
- Expanding the business
- Improving the quality of products/services
- Changing the type of business
- Penetrating new markets
- Diversifying the products/services
- Improving management style

In discussing how they would take these plans forward, the women entrepreneurs referred back to what they had listed as the major obstacles they faced in developing their business. Notably these related to the lack of working capital, the lack of managerial skills (especially negotiation skills), and problems with working and selling space, which all further hampered the development of their businesses (see Table 43 above).

(ii) Five Years Ahead

With regard to their short-term plans, nearly 60 per cent of the women micro and small-scale entrepreneurs stated that they believed they would still be operating the same business five years' time. As Table 44 shows, the remaining 40 per cent of women respondents were split equally between those that felt they would not be still operating if their current trend of businesses continued, and the others who weren't sure.

Table 44: The State of Business Ownership in Five Years' Time (by Business Category)

Category of Enterprise	Will Continue in the Same Business		Will Discontinue Current Business		Not Yet Decided	
	Frequency	%%	Frequency	%	Frequency	%
Micro	36	29.2	13	10.6	19	15.4
Small	37	30.1	12	9.8	6	4.9
All	**73**	**59.3**	**25**	**20.4**	**25**	**20.3**

Those women who felt that they would still be in the business gave the following – mostly positive – reasons for their statement:

- In order to expand the current business
- Having a strong affiliation with the business (attachment/affinity to the business)
- The business is growing and promising
- No other alternative available
- Satisfaction with the current business

Similarly, the women entrepreneurs that decided they would not be continuing with the same business also gave a mixed range of reasons for to their conclusion. They noted:

- Want to diversify products/services
- Business is not profitable
- Need to change the business and location
- Plan to look for other opportunities
- Will close this business due to high taxes and lack of market
- Plan to sell business

In summary, we note from this section of the report that in spite of the numerous challenges the women entrepreneurs faced while trying to develop their businesses, most of them have been succeeding in keeping them going. The majority of the women entrepreneurs appear to have been actively developing their businesses since start-up, they believe that their businesses are successful, and they have clear plans for the future and see themselves in their businesses five years hence. However, this does not mean that being self-employed is an easy or trouble-free economic option. In general, the women recognize that they have had their ups and downs, and that going into business is a challenge in itself. Whilst most of the women are engaged full-time in running their businesses, less than one-third pay themselves a regular wage. The women rely primarily on the re-investment of their profits to fund further business development. This might be a very prudent approach to business, but taking account of the women entrepreneurs' own views this clearly constrains such development and growth – often quoted as their greatest obstacles to further growth. Lastly, whilst the women entrepreneurs are gaining a great deal of experience by running their businesses, a significant number feel that they lack a range of managerial skills which may inhibit further growth.

3.4 Awareness and Use of Business Services

3.4.1 Awareness levels

Having looked at the women's businesses per se, the research also explored how aware and knowledgeable the women entrepreneurs were about the broader support and policy environment in which they were running their businesses. Table 45 indicates the women entrepreneurs' general awareness of the agencies and institutions providing various types of financial and business development services (BDS) support.

Table 45: Awareness of Business Support Institutions and Services

Business Support Agencies and Institutions	Awareness Levels		
	Micro %	Small %	Both %
Savings and credit services	47	42	44.7
Training in Small Business Management	32	35	33.3
Business Information	28	21	25.0
Indirect credit services	23	20	21.9
Marketing assistance	16	20	17.8
Networking	16	20	17.8
Provision of extension services	15	13	13.8
Technology assistance	8	11	9.7
Total numbers responding	**68**	**55**	**123 (100%)**

Overall their awareness is not particularly high, with the best known agencies being those associated with savings and credit services providers (44.7 per cent), training providers in small business management (33.3 per cent), and business information suppliers (25 per cent). Only 18 per cent of the women entrepreneurs knew organizations providing marketing assistance and only 10 per cent knew about technology support. The low level of awareness of support institutions, such as those providing marketing assistance and technology support, is mainly because such organizations are very weak or almost non-existent, and those which do exist do not actively promote their services to their target customers – and even les to women.

Those women entrepreneurs who know of and have used the services of such agencies are not particularly complimentary about the effectiveness of these service providers, particularly those engaged in credit operations like MFIs and banks.

As has been indicated earlier, the credit delivery modalities of the MFIs and the lending terms of the banks do not always meet the needs of both the small and microenterprise categories. Therefore, it is not surprising that the women entrepreneurs complain about the limited loan products of these agencies.

Non-financial support or BDS service providers, such as training providers, are known by many of the women entrepreneurs in both micro and small enterprises. However, most of the training provided in small business management is available mainly to microenterprise operators and is not available in every area. It would seem that training courses are not always based on identified needs, and this has been confirmed by the women entrepreneurs during the survey.

If women entrepreneurs are to get an adequate market for growth and expansion, there are opportunities for providing them with market information and promoting their products/services. The initiative taken by ILO's WEDGE team in facilitating 20-25 women micro-entrepreneurs to participate in Addis Ababa Exhibition and Bazaar was to help them to improve their market access, and such support is much needed. The women entrepreneurs' opinions about the training in exhibition skills (provided by the ILO and the Micro Enterprise Development Forum – MEDF) included the following comments[1]: the training helped to empower them economically and socially; many gained their first experience of a trade fair; for some of the women, it was the first time that they had stood alongside and competed with men entrepreneurs in a "market place"; many became aware of the need for better marketing communications,

---

[1] Barney-Gonzales, M. J. (2002).

promotional activities, and product design and development. However, on the negative side, some of the women commented that the sessions tended to be theoretical and not relevant to their specific problems; sometimes the training did not consider their educational background; the timing was not conducive as it conflicted with their business activities or with household chores, and the location of the training was not accessible.

Thus there is a challenge and opportunity for those designing and supplying appropriate non-financial support services for women entrepreneurs and for all those involved in the promotion of the micro and small enterprise economy in general and women entrepreneurs in particular. The issue of how appropriate the services are to meet the needs of the women entrepreneurs and their businesses would also seem to be an important point that must be addressed.

3.4.2 Affiliation with Business and Women's Organizations

Entrepreneurial business associations or chambers of commerce can be a major force for entrepreneurs in helping them to address common problems and lobby the government and other bodies for the general and specific improvements to the business environment. These associations and networks can also be used to address specific issues, problems, barriers and disadvantages affecting women entrepreneurs.

The women entrepreneurs were asked if they were members of any associations. Less than a third of the women (31 per cent) who responded (n = 115) are affiliated to an organization. A slightly higher number of small-scale entrepreneurs (32.6 per cent) were members than the micro-entrepreneurs (27.9 per cent). Women were then asked to name organizations of which they were members. Table 46 shows the main organizations to which the women are affiliated with the Women Entrepreneurs Association being the most popular (45 per cent), followed by the Chambers of Commerce (30 per cent).

Table 46: Organizations to which Women Entrepreneurs are Affiliated

Organizations	Micro %	Small %	Both %
Women Entrepreneurs' Associations	33	13	46
Chamber of Commerce	9	21	30
Women Entrepreneurs' Association and Chambers of Commerce	9	6	15
Women Exporters' Forum	3	6	9
Total	**54**	**46**	**100**

Women engaged in microenterprises are mainly affiliated with the recently established Women Entrepreneurs Associations (33 per cent), whereas women engaged in small-scale business are mainly involved in Chambers of Commerce (21 per cent).

This relatively low membership of women entrepreneurs in such organizations may be due to their lack of awareness about the existence of these organizations and the benefits that membership can bring. From the survey it seems that associations are sometimes considered as political structures for controlling or regulating businesses.

Women entrepreneurs and others seem to be cautious about joining associations because they have not had a good experience with them or have heard negative reports from others. During the Derg regime, women in Ethiopia were mobilized and forced to join such groups and pay monthly membership fees for over 15 years, and yet they did not get any tangible benefit as members. Later, after the change of government a women's association called Ethiopian Women Entrepreneurs' Association was established, but it seems to have had little impact.

The women entrepreneurs in the case studies all indicated that they are not members of any associations currently. Some of them were members of the Chambers of Commerce but left because they did not get any benefits from membership. Therefore, it appears that it is not only lack of awareness that is keeping women entrepreneurs from registering as members of associations, but also the lack of benefits – be this actual and perceived.

Women engaged in small-scale enterprises received moderate support in networking (14 per cent) and obtaining market information (11 per cent) in comparison to those engaged in microenterprise activities. This is mainly because small enterprises that are licensed can easily be accepted as members of the chambers of commerce. As has been explained by the women entrepreneurs in the survey, the regional women entrepreneurs' associations are young organizations that have evolved just few years ago as legal entities and, therefore, are not yet in a position to provide effective services to members until they are strengthened through different capacity building programmes. One good example is the training provided by the ILO in November 2002 for more than 25 members and representatives of associations and NGOs on capacity building on women's entrepreneurship development.

Despite the low rate of membership, almost all of the women entrepreneurs who are members of women entrepreneurs' associations and chambers of commerce said that they have positive attitudes to these organizations. They said that they are important in addressing common problems, facilitating training, providing relevant information, speaking on behalf of key women entrepreneurs' questions, advocating for positive policy responses, and lobbying on their behalf.

3.4.3 Women Entrepreneurs' Awareness of Policy Issues

An attempt has been made to record the awareness level of women entrepreneurs of government policies and regulations related to women and their businesses. The women were asked about a series of recent policy measures concerning micro and small enterprises and women in Ethiopia so as to gauge their awareness and understanding of these measures. The research showed that:

- 54 per cent of the women entrepreneurs are aware of '*The Proclamation on Trade Registration and Licensing*'
- 25 per cent are aware of' *the Micro-Finance Institutions Proclamation*'
- 24 per cent are aware of '*the National Policy on Ethiopian Women*'
- 16 per cent are aware of '*the National Micro and Small Enterprises Development Strategy*'

From this it can be said that women entrepreneurs have some awareness of government policies related to their businesses. Trade registration and licensing policies seem to be the areas that women know well and have benefited from, as they are the owners of registered businesses. The National Micro and Small Enterprises

Development Strategy is known to only 16 per cent of the women entrepreneurs. This indicates that the strategy needs more popularization to be able to benefit women entrepreneurs engaged in the sector, and for whom the strategy was designed. When the women were asked, "Do you think the present policy environment discriminates against women?", 78 per cent of those responding (n=121) felt that the policy environment does not discriminate against women, with only 10 per cent feeling it did.

Although it is often mentioned that Ethiopian laws and policies in general appear to be gender neutral in content, some of the women indicated that the policies are discriminatory against women in both content and meaning. Others pointed out that the discrimination occurs at the level of implementation. In fact, 34 per cent of women entrepreneurs interviewed responded that changes and improvements in Government policy alone would not help businesses to grow, because much of the problem is lack of proper implementation of the various policies that are instigated from time to time. They also suggested that there should be improvement in the attitude of the public towards women entrepreneurs, and that they should be considered as important contributors to economic and social development in Ethiopia.

In response to the question, "Can you mention specific changes in the business environment now, since Government promised to implement certain measures to assist women entrepreneurs?", 13 per cent of the women entrepreneurs responded positively and 87 per cent negatively. When this is further considered by category, 89 per cent of micro-entrepreneurs said they have not noticed changes in the business environment, while 11 per cent indicated that they have seen some positive changes, such as the introduction of market-based economic system in the country.

4. Case Studies on Experiences of Women in Growing Businesses

In order to draw lessons from and better illustrate the experiences of women in growing businesses, five enterprises were identified for case studies: three are small enterprises whilst the other two are microenterprises. The first case relates to the experience of Byogenic Beauty Spot, providing aesthetic skin-care; the second looks at the experience of a women with a bakery business, and the third entrepreneur has a printing press business. Of the two microenterprise cases, the first considers the experience of a woman with a disability who sells religious items near churches as well as making handicrafts, and the second examines the situation of a young woman entrepreneur running a tailoring training centre. The case studies show a range of very different backgrounds in entering into business, as well as of their experiences of developing their businesses.

4.1 Case Studies on Growth-oriented Small Enterprises

4.1.1 Mrs. Mulumebet G/Sellassie of Byogenic Beauty Spot (BBS)

Mrs Mulumebet G/Sellassie, who is in her mid-40s, was like many women entrepreneurs, employed by others before deciding to start her own business. After graduating from the Addis Ababa Commercial College, she joined a Government organization where she worked as an Export Manager for five years. In order to develop her experience and career, she left the agency to work for another five years as an Executive Secretary with an international Non Governmental Organization (NGO).

Following her marriage, Mrs Mulumebet stopped working for the NGO and planned to realize her childhood dream to be self-employed and earn her own income by establishing a Beauty Centre. Following a one-year training course in the United States of America, and six-months training in the Netherlands, and with financial support from her husband as well as from her own savings, in 1993 she opened a business called Byogenic Beauty Spot. The services provided by Byogenic Beauty Spot (BBS) include skin-care services including facials, waxing, eye treatment, electrolysis, thermal body wrap, massage, sun pigment removal and semi-permanent make-up.

When reflecting on the business Mrs Mulumebet said ,"I enjoy very strong support from my husband in financial and other terms, including caring for the kids, and support and advice on business matters".

She recalls the tough challenges she faced at the start of her business. "At the beginning, I faced obstacles in finding working premises, bureaucratic red-tape in obtaining licences and importing my equipment, lack of credit facilities from banks, and problems in obtaining land. Later on, the main problem became accessing the market, as the business idea was new to Ethiopia". She had serious marketing difficulties for about half a year, as the services she provides were not fully understood, and customers thought she was simply offering another beauty salon or hairdressing service.

She rented a villa as her working premises and promoted her business using flyers, posters, and word of mouth. She recognized that her customers would include those from foreign communities living in Addis Ababa, as they were more likely to be familiar with the services she offered. In addition, she wished to target Ethiopians in the higher income bracket. Mrs Mulumebet also planned her marketing to promote her business through newspapers, giving seminars to community schools, and through the Science and Technology Commission. From all of this she felt she succeeded in introducing her new business and building her customer base.

The business is a sole proprietorship established in 1993, with an original capital outlay of Birr 350,000 (USD 41,176) and initially employing two workers. After nine years trading, the company has developed to a small-scale enterprise with a capital base of Birr 1.5 million (USD 176,471) and providing employment for 22 persons, of which 16 are female workers. Her employees receive regular salary increases and annual bonuses as well as commissions. Mrs Mulumebet feels that these are important tools for increasing productivity and ensuring employee motivation and, therefore, in turn contributing to customer satisfaction.

In expanding her business, Mrs Mulumebet feels that the main problems she faced were a lack of skilled human resources, difficulty in getting land/space; problems in accessing training; bureaucratic red tape when dealing with the tax office; and lack of easy access to credit. In order to address these problems, Mrs Mulumebet devised a range of strategies. She developed a programme of on-the-job training for her workers. She also extended the rented house and made use of every inch of space for the expansion needs of her business.

She said, "due to the lack of collateral and virtual absence of appreciation of my business by the banks, as it is often considered as simple hair dressing, banks were not willing to extend credit to me". Thus, she had to rely on the profits generated from the enterprise and plough these back to fund expansion and diversification of her business.

Mrs Mulumebet states that her business is unique in that no-one else is supplying this service in Addis Ababa. In order to stay ahead of the market and ensure high quality of service, Mrs Mulumebet takes part in training every two years and participates in international professional conferences. In order to broaden her knowledge, she has established contacts with international organizations and receives monthly professional journals and training manuals which she uses continuously for training herself and her employees. In discussion, Mrs Mulumebet said that she is not aware of the availability of support services for business development in Ethiopia.

Mrs Mulumebet believes that there is a good opportunity for her business as long as there are skilled persons to do the job. She sought to diversify her contacts and markets, and is now managing the health club of the Addis Ababa Hilton Hotel. This experience has encouraged her to negotiate to manage and operate health clubs in other hotels. She also participates in special events and fashion shows, and renders her professional know-how in make-up and beautification services and has clients coming from as far as Nazareth and Dire Dawa.

Mrs Mulumebet is forward looking and is planning to establish her own training centre to address the problem of a lack of trained personnel in the sector. She believes that this would help create opportunities for employment, income generation and transfer of know-how, as well as complementing on-the-job training and contributing to skills upgrading. Her business will also offer opportunities for the trainees to set up their own businesses.

Mrs Mulumebet is not a member of any women entrepreneurs' association or any chamber of commerce in Ethiopia, but she believes in networking for business development and actively tries to broaden her own network. Mrs Mulumebet is aware of Government policies. She does not believe that women are discriminated against however, but she pointed out the lack of implementation of Government policy for both women and men, as indicated in the survey findings.

In sharing her experiences, Mrs Mulumebet said "to be successful, women entrepreneurs need to have clear objectives and vision, and the strength and determination to achieve them. She also said "the growth of Ethiopian women entrepreneurs is hampered among others by their poor educational background, lack of exposure and cultural barriers. These problems, have seriously affected the level of confidence of many women to engage in new fields of growth-oriented businesses." She also underlines the importance of giving personal attention to the business and its customers, as well as to following up and managing daily activities to satisfy customers as vital elements for the success of business enterprises.

Mrs Mulumebet has two children: a boy (14) and a girl (12). She said that her children have begun assisting her in her business activities by preparing flyers and posters.

4.1.2 Mrs. Semret Abate – Mulbul Bakery

Semret Abate comes from a middle-class family in Addis Ababa and was the only daughter among five boys. Upon graduation from the Commercial School of Addis Ababa in 1988, she joined an NGO as a secretary. She was working with the NGO when she married her ex-husband who was then a businessman, but they are now divorced.

From the very beginning, Semret wished to be independent through working for herself. Using the skills she learned at the Commercial School, she opened a small typing school in a rented Kebele house (the lowest local administration) in Addis Ababa. At the time, she didn't have much in savings and she had to borrow a small amount of money from her mother to buy six old typewriters.

Semret remembers that when her husband heard about her intention to start a typing school, he was not happy about it. He wanted her to stay at home because he believed that his income was enough to provide for the family. Nonetheless, she continued with her own plans and established the typing school. She was eager to expand the business and was therefore saving whatever money she earned from the business. Within a short period of time, she expanded the typing school facilities by buying new electric typewriters and computers. The number of the students increased to 200 at the end of the second year.

"I was happy about running the school because I made every decision about the business on my own and I felt I had built my self-confidence as well. However, my husband was trying to demoralize me by belittling my achievements. I remember one day when my family was watching the TV and an advert for my typing school came on. The whole family was excited, but my husband was negative being against my idea of advertising the business. He even mentioned that I was wasting my time and money by investing in the advertisement."

After operating the typing school for three years, she started searching for new business ideas, as she could not expand the typing school further due to space restrictions. She felt that an import business might be a viable venture, and so using the profits she generated from the typing school and from the sale of the assets of the school she started an import business. She converted the typing school premises to an office and used her mother's house as a store for the imported goods.

Although at the beginning she was mainly importing textile products, such as bed-spreads, later on she added new items like carbon papers, razor blades, etc. She did this upon the suggestion of her customers. She was doing well when her business was interrupted by the war between Ethiopia and Eritrea in 2000. At the time she awaiting the delivery of items she had ordered. The goods were already at Assab Port when the war started, and they were confiscated by the Eritrean Government. Unfortunately, she only received a small delivery that later came through the Djibouti Port. The value of the goods she received via Djibouti Port was so small that she was at a loss as to how to continue supporting her children.

While she was in the import business, she had an opportunity to travel to different developed and developing countries. Her last trip was to Syria to claim the small items that did not arrive at Assab Port when the war started. On this particular trip, she had a chance to explore the possibility of going into a bakery business.

Since she had lost almost all of her money in the import business, it was difficult for her to go into the bakery business immediately by raising new capital. Towards the end of 2000, she was able to establish the bakery business partly by borrowing money from individuals she knew – but at an exorbitantly high interest rate. The start-up capital was Birr 100,000 (USD 11,765). Currently the business, excluding the building, is worth over Birr 250,000 (USD 29,412).

Although she said the process was very long, she was able to access a loan amounting to Birr 100,000 (USD 11,765) from one of the private commercial banks. The loan was a short-term loan repayable within 12 months. Her mother agreed to allow her house to be used as collateral. She felt that the monthly repayment was very high for the bakery business as the profit is low.

Semret did not have the skills to run the bakery business when she started, she hired someone (an expert) from the country where she imported the machinery. At the beginning she did everything herself with the assistance of the expert. She delivered bread to different hotels and restaurants, and she was the purchaser, manager, accountant and cashier. After three months, she employed five workers. Now the bakery business provides employment to 30 persons and has five sales outlets in Addis Ababa. She has fully repaid the first loan with interest and is up-to-date in her tax payments. She has again taken a short-term loan from another private bank, although the monthly repayments do sometimes cause her cash flow difficulties.

Semret indicated that the banks do not take into consideration the cash flow of the business and, therefore her ability to repay the loan. The length of the repayment period for short-term loans for any type of enterprise is the same regardless of the type of business. She stated that it is only if the bakery is in mass production and distribution that it is possible to sustain the business and repay loans. On the other hand, to go into mass production or enhance the economies of scale, she claims that she needs a considerable amount of working capital and that is not facilitated by the banks for various reasons.

"I haven't seen or heard of any bank that gives special treatment for women entrepreneurs who try their level best to be self-employed and take part in the development of their country, in addition to their reproductive work bestowed upon them by tradition or culture. Bureaucracy sometimes stifles creativity and innovation. You don't get quick answers to your queries. Even the banks do not dare to shorten the lending process. They shorten only their loan repayment periods to get back their money somehow, without giving due consideration for the encouragement and development of women entrepreneurs, or without any understanding of the general environment under which we operate."

Semret stated that she has never received any business support such as training or technical advice from any source. She was a member of the Chamber of Commerce of Addis Ababa while she was in the import business, but feels that she did not see any tangible benefit from being a member. Currently, she is not a member of any business association. The problem, she said, is that it is difficult for a women entrepreneur who is struggling to make ends meet to identify who is who in the provision of business support. She felt that these organizations do not advertise their services adequately.

Semret feels that because she is self-employed, she can provide for her children and makes her own decisions. She feels empowered and self-confident now, and that satisfies her. She said she follows her own instincts in making her business decisions. There is nobody who can say "I told you not to" when there is something wrong, and she feels that this is very important for her.

She emphasized that although the road to entrepreneurship is not easy, women should have the endurance and should not loose hope easily. They should be creative and do something others haven't done; something that is challenging but is rewarding rather than copying things others are doing. With the earnings from her business, she supports seven household members including her three children. Semret considers her mother as her role model who she said is even now, in her old age, is running a restaurant in the United States.

4.1.3 Romane Demissi – Rome Printing Press

Romane Demissie was born and raised in Awassa, southern Ethiopia, 50 years ago. Her parents were a relatively well-to-do family who moved to Addis Ababa in the early sixties. The eldest of 10 sisters and brothers, Romane went to school for five years, but her parents decided that she should quit school at that stage and marry. Romane was very unhappy. They told her that she didn't need further education because her husband and her family could provide for whatever she needed to lead a happy married life".

She married her husband in 1961, but towards the end of 1977 they were divorced. Just a little before they were divorced, there was change of government and the Derg regime nationalized land and confiscated the houses and other properties belonging to her parents and her husband. She and her four children didn't have anything to live on. Romane moved in with her grandparents who were living in a small house.

With the assistance of her relatives and using her small savings, she started a small flour mill business in her grandparents' house. "I didn't have any idea how to run a business. I was doing it through trial and error. I struggled for almost nine years to run the flourmill and then went bankrupt."

Immediately after the flourmill closed she started supplying 'Enjera'[2] to a hotel on contract basis. With her savings from the sale of 'Enjera' she modified the house that was earlier used as a flourmill and converted it to a small hotel. Because she came from a wealthy family some people were not happy about her going into the hotel business. She said, "it was a blessing in disguise that my father died a little earlier before I went into a hotel business. He could have objected to the idea and may have severed our relations as a result." She pointed out that during earlier times, people thought that for a woman, going into a hotel business was tantamount to working as a prostitute.

She remembers that when people who are close friends of her family came to her small hotel, she used to hide behind doors so that she would not be humiliated by the comments they would have made, thinking that she disgraced the family by engaging in a hotel business.

While running the hotel she had her difficulties, partly because she could not get title deed to the house her grandparents gave her, and she couldn't expand the hotel due to lack of finance. Nonetheless, with the income from the hotel she was able to educate all of her children who are now abroad.

After operating the hotel for six years, she leased it to an individual and left for the United States to take care of her children and remained there for four years. When she returned, she started exploring new business ideas and after contacting some professional people who were friends of her deceased brother, she decided to set up a printing business. In 1999, using the proceeds from the lease of her small hotel, she established a printing press in the same house that had been used as a hotel before. "Since I didn't have printing skills and there were no institutions that provided training on printing, I tried to get some ideas by going around and talking to people who had knowledge of the printing business. I started with one small second hand printing machine and accessories and with four employees."

Currently, she has nine employees and two small printing machines with complete accessories. Her total assets, she estimates, are now about Birr 400,000 (USD 47,060). She said that although she wants to expand the business, lack of finance makes it difficult. She runs the business by ploughing back the profit, but cannot borrow from banks because she cannot offer suitable collateral, as she still does not have title deed to her house.

---

[2] Traditional Ethiopian bread/pancake.

Space is also a problem and limits any expansion plans, because she uses part of the premises as a residence for herself and the six household members that she supports. She has tried to rent an additional house but has not been successful.

She manages the business and is happy with this, although due to lack of technical capacity things sometimes go wrong. For example, she spent a large amount of money buying an accessory, which was not compatible with her existing printing machine. "I don't have any role model in my life. I went into self-employment for survival and to support my children because I was a single mother. Because of my family background I was not exposed to the outer world or my surroundings. I was just taking risks to survive, and thanks to God I got my children somewhere because I was able to provide for them by being self-employed."

Although she has no savings, she tries to meet the working capital of the business at the current level by ploughing back the profit. She plans to expand or add some machinery if she is able to access a bank loan.

Romane emphasized the importance of women being organized to overcome the problems that impinge upon their efforts to play a full part in the development of their country. She feels that there are few associations that aim to support women entrepreneurs. Romane was a member of the Chamber of Commerce of Addis Ababa when she was operating the flourmill enterprise, but left because she felt she did not benefit in any way from membership. Currently, she does not belong to any business association.

She said that men dominate the printing sector and, because of her background she is sometimes not bold enough to negotiate and also feels she lacks the skills of persuasion which is an important aspect of running businesses, such as printing. To compensate for her weaknesses in these areas, she has now employed a salesperson on permanent basis.

Romane is of the opinion that the government and society in general has the responsibility to provide an enabling environment for women entrepreneurs who, regardless of all the odds, are trying to be self-employed and support themselves and their families. She stated that young women should try to run their own businesses and they should not shy away because they have to start small and from scratch. She feels that it is only if they make efforts to positively change themselves that women entrepreneurs will change the perception of the society towards women.

4.2   Case Studies of Microenterprises

4.2.1 Ms. Mekdes Abebe, Handicrafts

Mekdes Abebe, who was born in one of the northern administrative regions called Gojjam, is the sixteenth child of her parents. Her father is a wealthy lawyer but her mother died while Mekdes was very young. She is now 29 years old and is a micro-entrepreneur who provides for herself and cares for four of her brother's abandoned children.

Mekdes has a severe physical disability that means she cannot walk around and relies on a wheelchair. Her experiences of disability have had a profound impact upon her life.

'I was born healthy, but my parents told me that when I was just a baby, I fell down and some part of my body was damaged. Initially I was half-paralyzed below my waist then, gradually, it resulted in my total paralysis. My parents thought it was a curse. Just my existence around the house made them uncomfortable and they pretended to themselves and the community that I simply was not there. I was never allowed to go out of the house, and when a visitor came, they tried to keep me out of sight. I was not allowed to go to school and that always used to offend me.'

People with disabilities in Ethiopia are vulnerable not just because of their disability, but also because of the attitudes towards disability. According to traditional beliefs in many parts of Ethiopia, disability has a supernatural origin. Disability symbolizes a curse, which has struck a particular person, but is most likely a big burden on the whole family. As a result, those afflicted by disabilities tend to be shunned by society, while their families try to keep them hidden.

At around age 10, Mekdes started rebelling against her parents' attitudes towards her. She wanted to get an education but she was denied the opportunity. Upon her persistence and insistence, they allowed her to undertake some activities that would not take her away from the house. She started performing some embroidery work on different national costumes and charging small amounts of money for this service. Through this she was able to save about Birr 1,000 (USD 118). At the time, and in addition to her disability, she also had health problems, but nobody cared to take her to a hospital. Later on, with the assistance of a relative, she got a supporting letter from Kebele (the lowest local administrative unit) to get medical treatment free of charge in Addis Ababa. Using her savings, she left home for Addis Ababa without the knowledge of her parents.

In Addis Ababa, she was admitted to the Black Lion Hospital, where she was operated on and then hospitalized for over one year. While in the hospital, she used to collect disposed plastic bags and knitted these into baskets that she used to sell to the hospital community, such as patients, visitors, etc. In one year she had earned Birr 500 (USD 59) from this activity. When she left the hospital she used this money to buy an old wheelchair. Since she had nowhere to go, upon leaving the hospital she stayed in a church compound in the centre of Addis. After a while and with the assistance of a church member, she was allowed to use a small hut that was at the rear of the church. She used to sustain herself by producing and selling large bags to groceries around the church.

She also recommenced doing embroidery on bedspreads, pillows, etc., although her customers were mainly people who just wanted to help her. At the same time she started evening classes and completed grade 8. Mekdes considers this as one of her greatest achievements.

Through a friend working in an NGO, Mekdes was assisted to work for the NGO by doing and selling embroidery. She was paid on piece-rate basis for this work, and the amount depended on the volumes of sales. The pay was low and so she left the NGO after a year.

Mekdes recommenced working for herself. She was thrilled with joy when the NGO gave her a sewing machine on credit. She also borrowed money for working capital. The two loans were repaid within a year. She diversified her activities. On religious holidays she sold incense, candles, religious books, newspapers and umbrellas (special ones used by churches) by going to different churches, depending on the specific saint's day. During working days, she stayed at home working on her embroidery and producing candles.

'I do my domestic work myself like any typical Ethiopian woman. I do not want the children to miss school for the sake of assisting me in household chores.' said Mekdes.

After living in the church compound for 13 years, she got a positive answer to her 11-year application to rent a Government (public sector) house from a Kebele. It is after this that she started assisting her brother's abandoned four children. Two of these children have now made it to high school. She also made some improvements in her rented house so that it creates a more conducive environment for the children to study, including having a telephone line installed. She says that sometimes the telephone is a lifeline for her.

Mekdes is a very well-organised woman. She plans everything ahead of time. For instance, she decides to access loans only after she has correctly identified her needs for working capital. Using the loan money, she buys all her raw materials in bulk and for a year's consumption. She has started accessing working capital loans from a micro-finance institution (MFI) that operates near her residence. The last loan she took was Birr 2,500 (USD 295). She also maintains a savings deposit with the MFI. 'If I keep the loan money on hand, I do not know what emergencies might take place and force me to use it for unproductive things. So I prepare everything in advance before I take the loan money, and when the money is available I immediately utilize it for the intended purposes'.

Mekdes manages her money so well that for every telephone call she makes from her home, she puts the coin in the box prepared for the purpose and when the bill comes, she uses the deposited money to settle it.

Mekdes is full of ideas and continues to plan to diversify her products. Her major problem now is lack of sales outlets for some of her products. She has applied to the Kebele to allow her to have a piece of land on which she can construct a shop. However, she says she may not get an answer so easily, like all of the other micro-entrepreneurs.

Mekdes says that, "to be an entrepreneur it does not matter to be a man or woman, it is the aptitude, the interest to work for oneself and the commitment that matters."

4.2.2 Belainesh Eshetu – Betel Tailoring Training Centre

Belainesh Eshetu was born and raised in Addis Ababa. The fourth child of her parents, she is 24 years of age and dropped out of grade ten due to personal reasons. After her mother died when Belainesh was a small girl, she was forced to live with her aunt who was also a poor women living only on her husband's meagre income. The living conditions in her aunt's family deteriorated further when her husband, who was the only bread-earner, died leaving behind four children.

Belainesh remembers that one day when she came back from school her aunt's family had nothing to eat. "After thinking for a while, I decided to ask my brother for money to help my aunt and her children. He gave me a very small amount of money (less than Birr 20), and I used part of it to buy food for that day and decided to use the remainder on something that would generate some sort of income for the family. I bought wheat flour and baked ambasha (local bread) and sold it to people around our living areas – that is how I started business."

She continued selling food, such as 'Enjera', and sometimes she prepared food and drinks during her spare time and her aunt sold it around their home. Later when she finished schooling she went back to her father. Upon her suggestion her father sent her to a sewing school. Because the father's income was low, Belainesh remembers that sometimes when he could not pay the monthly training fee, she stopped attendance but ultimately managed to complete the two-year training. With the assistance of her older brother she was able to buy an old sewing machine, and with that she started doing some embroidery work which she sold mainly to her neighbours and relatives.

Although her intention was to establish a tailoring centre/school, Belainesh couldn't buy additional sewing machines due to her lack of financial resources, and it was impossible to get working premises to start the business.

Belainesh says she tried several places to get financial and other support services. "I wanted to be self-employed or go into something that is worth doing by using the skills I acquired. However, I really didn't know how to go about it. One day I talked to the Kebele officials about renting space where I can start my own business. The Kebele told me about the NGO called WISE (Women in Self Employment) – it was my lucky day". She took part in a training programme offered by the NGO. The training included marketing, record-keeping and money management. After the training, she took loans to buy additional sewing machines. The NGO lobbied the Kebele to allow it to build working sheds for its beneficiaries on a piece of land around the same area. Belainesh was lucky enough to get a small shed as a working space. In 1999, she established a tailoring school, and currently she has four sewing machines and employs a young woman to assist her in the training business.

After starting the business Belainesh left her parent's house and rented a house of her own. She remembers how her family were furious when she told them that she wanted to be close to her business area. Regardless of their opposition, she moved out, and now she supports herself and her two sisters who are both attending college.

Belainesh feels empowered because she can decide about her own affairs on her own. "While I was attending the sewing class most of my friends where mocking about my misery. Now I am sorry for them because they are still unemployed in their late twenties and are still dependent on their parents."

Belainesh has a plan to legalize her business by obtaining a licence. She said that formalizing the business would help her to operate freely without the fear that the authorities would come and force her to close down because she is not licensed.

However, she is worried because it is difficult to find a suitable working place at a fairly low rent. The current working place is not suitable for her business. She said she could not take the risk of moving to other areas where the rent is extremely high. She is worried that she might go bankrupt. The problem of finance is another constraint she mentioned. Although she has the skills and interest to engage in producing and selling more refined products like wedding dresses which could earn her more income, she cannot pursue these due to lack of additional finance and suitable working and selling space.

The loan given by the NGO was very small for the type of work she aspired to go into. She cannot access bank loans due to the fact that she lacks fixed assets to offer as collateral. "I have the know-how and interest in the work, however, creativity without finance and other facilities is of no use in any business."

Although she does not belong to any business association or women's organizations, the NGO organizes women into groups to access loans and other support services. Through this, she said that we have a chance to exchange ideas about our businesses during their weekly meetings.

Belainesh asserts that due to the chronic unemployment in the country, young school-leavers remain dependent on their families and later on when they see no alternatives some go out in the streets as prostitutes. The community, NGOs, government and all concerned should come together to create the opportunity for these young women to be self-employed and lead a productive life. She believes that the women need organizations that would lobby for an enabling environment and show them how to engage themselves productively.

She stated that young Ethiopian women should open their eyes and look out for alternatives, rather than remaining at home indefinitely and depend on their parents who have suffered enough to bring them to the level they are at now.

5. Summary of the Major Findings

The primary research has provided a broad range of information on women entrepreneurs and women-operated enterprises, and on the problems and opportunities facing women entrepreneurs in Ethiopia. The research has also contributed to a greater understanding and knowledge of the experiences of women's business growth, the business support framework, and the broader environment within which women's businesses operate in Ethiopia. The team of national consultants prepared the following major findings arising from the fieldwork investigations, and also on the basis of the earlier preliminary report.

5.1 Regional Divergence

Although the survey was carried out in six different major towns of six regional states, including Addis Ababa, there appears to be no major differences in the way the women start and develop their businesses or in the overall enabling or support environment. There are no significant observed differences between the land lease policies and availability of premises in these major towns. One observed difference between Addis Ababa and the rest of the five towns is that as Addis Ababa is a major (capital) city, the population is larger and therefore offers greater market opportunities. Gender inequalities appear to be the same in the major towns.

5.2 General Characteristics of the Women Entrepreneurs and their Enterprises

The findings of the primary research and the in-depth interviews indicate that the majority of women entrepreneurs (87 per cent) are less than 49 years of age; 89 per cent were either married, divorced or widowed, and most have attained secondary level of schooling. The average household size was found to be 6 persons, as compared to the national average of 4.85 persons.

The research also confirmed that the major motivating factors for women to start their own businesses were to support their families, to be self-employed, and to generate their own income. The survey results showed that 44 per cent are engaged in services, 30 per cent in trade, 15 per cent in production, and the remaining 11 per cent in both trade and handicrafts.

In more than half of the cases (57 per cent) the initiation of the business idea for the enterprise came from the woman herself. The women did not face any significant negative reactions in establishing these businesses, as 65 per cent of spouses and 62 per cent of other family members were supportive of their business ideas.

5.3 Financial and Non-financial Resources

5.3.1 Financial Resources

The survey indicated that the main sources for the start-up and expansion of women-operated enterprises came from personal savings and family loans/contributions. This has proved to be a constraint for some women entrepreneurs, especially when trying to mobilize adequate working capital for expanding or diversifying the business.

Although savings are one of the means of accumulation of capital, many women entrepreneurs reported that savings alone were not always sufficient for running and expanding their business operations. The growth of the enterprises can be restricted due to a lack of finance for working capital and for long-term capital investments. The women entrepreneurs found it very difficult to access credit from banks due to the requirements of the banks, such as the collateral, the expected level of contribution from the women entrepreneurs themselves, and from MFIs due to the low loan ceiling, and the inconvenient lending and repayment arrangements.

5.3.2 Non-financial Resources

The majority of women entrepreneurs (60 per cent) have experienced difficulties in finding and acquiring land and premises for production or provision of services, as well as for selling purposes. Most run their businesses from rented premises, but the relatively high rents poses critical problems for them and can hinder their expansion and diversification.

The vast majority of women entrepreneurs market their products and services to their local markets, which for most means a limited market access. Very few of the small-scale and growth-oriented enterprises sell at regional markets. This shows that there is limited exploration of market development into new markets, which should bring better price advantages. Because of these reasons, many of the women entrepreneurs are engaged in stiff competition with each another for the same small local markets, and this inevitably results in lower returns all round.

The potential for market development is also limited since many of the women are engaged in similar types of businesses. Many of these business sectors are traditionally dominated by women for historical and socio-cultural reasons. The mobility of some of the women entrepreneurs is also restricted by family responsibilities and cultural barriers, and this contrives to limit their access to wider markets.

Most of the women entrepreneurs sell their products directly to consumers, and few market through intermediaries such as wholesalers. The limited linkages between the women micro-entrepreneurs and the medium and large businesses also mean that their opportunities are limited for networking and growth.

Women entrepreneurs use a narrow range of promotional methods with the majority use word of mouth and signboards to advertise their products/services. Advertising, using exhibitions, distributing flyers and business cards are not well used by the women entrepreneurs. Once again, this is partly due to their lack of promotional know-how and partly their lack of resources.

Many women entrepreneurs lack access to adequate business development services (BDS), although organizations such as WISE, GTZ, UNIDO and Enterprise Ethiopia, as well as the ILO, are redoubling their efforts in this regard. The reasons indicated for this are: a low level of awareness about service providers, and some women entrepreneurs themselves are not accustomed to seeking and obtaining such support services. There also seems to be only a limited range of services available that are tailored to the specific needs of women entrepreneurs.

5.4 Managerial Capacity of the Women Entrepreneurs

It was clear from the survey that women entrepreneurs manage their enterprises with support from family and friends, both at start-up and expansion. Use of external, formal, managerial capacity-building support by women entrepreneurs is very limited.

5.5 Networking

The women entrepreneurs' associations are mainly young organizations, and at present they do not appear to be very strong and do not meet the full range of needs of the women entrepreneurs. Membership levels are low and some of the women entrepreneurs do not feel that there would be real benefits from joining. This position presents challenges for the (new) associations, to see how they can strengthen and build their services and promote themselves in a better and more efficient manner.

5.6 Decision-making

The findings of the field survey indicated that the majority of women entrepreneurs make their own independent decisions on the utilization of money generated from their businesses, as well as on matters that affect their business. In addition, it was noted that a significant number of the women surveyed who operate small enterprises make joint decisions with their husbands when the decision involves complex matters or where the husband's permission is required – for example offering their joint property as collateral or disposing of a major property.

5.7 Awareness Level of Government Policies

The primary research showed that there appears to be an adequate level of awareness among women entrepreneurs about government policies that concern their businesses. According to the survey, most of the women entrepreneurs think that changes are required to create a more conducive environment for their respective operations and to facilitate the growth of their enterprises. In particular, most have mentioned that the tax system needs a significant improvement, as the existing tax laws, which now levy taxes on the basis of estimates, do not consider the ability of small businesses to pay taxes.

5.8 Differences between Micro and Small Enterprises

As far as access to resources or support services is concerned, both the micro and small enterprise categories seem to face the same constraints at start-up and during the growth stage of their enterprises. Because of the nature of activities and the level of capital invested, the small enterprises have generated more employment than the microenterprises.

6.   Proposed Interventions

The team of national consultants, Zewde & Associates, prepared the preliminary report in which the secondary information on women entrepreneurs in Ethiopia was reviewed[3]. Following the identification of key questions which required further investigation in the fieldwork stage, the national consultants conducted interviews with 123 women entrepreneurs, as well as 5 in-depth interviews with other women entrepreneurs. Using the findings from the secondary and primary research stages as their basis, the national consultants proposed a set of supportive interventions aimed at promoting and assisting women entrepreneurs in Ethiopia. These proposals for support formed a valuable part of the entire research exercise led by the ILO in Ethiopia, and they were presented in a general way to the ILO's national conference on women entrepreneurs, held in November 2002. They also stimulated the consultative participatory process at the national conference, and informed the discussions leading to the set of conference recommendations as shown in section 7 below.

The primary research showed that women entrepreneurs have important potential and opportunities for growth. But they lack certain facilities and are facing various constraints, and this situation has restricted their prospects for growth. In the interventions proposed by the team of national consultants to promote women entrepreneurs in Ethiopia, it is suggested that they should focus mainly on those who have growth potential and are engaged in small-scale enterprises in particular, in order to achieve meaningful employment creation through this sector. The proposed interventions are grouped under a number of headings as shown below.

6.1   Financial Institutions

Limited access to the credit services of banks and MFIs has been identified as one of the key constraints facing women entrepreneurs. Banks and micro-finance institutions should review their loan products for the women entrepreneurs in growth-oriented micro and small enterprises. In undertaking this review, the banks and MFIs should consider:

- Allocating certain portions of their loanable funds for women entrepreneurs who are planning to grow their business;
- Designing alternative collateral systems that take account of the women's economic position, as well as the development and financial requirements of their enterprises:
- Lowering the level of the banks' required contribution from women entrepreneurs, at least for those at start-up stage;
- Greater collaboration and networking among MFIs and banks so that women entrepreneurs who outgrow the financial services of MFIs could be directed to banks for higher loans.

---

[3] Zewde & Associates (2002).

6.2   Role of Government

6.2.1 Enabling Environment

It is very important that the regulatory framework that affects business activities in general, and those influencing women entrepreneurs in particular, be revised regularly to create a more conducive and enabling environment. In this regard, the tax system needs proper attention as almost all women entrepreneurs have complaints over the existing subjective method of the tax levy assessment, which is based on subjective estimates and which does not take account of the ability of the enterprises to meet the tax demands.

6.2.2 Credit Facilities

Following the proposals in 6.1 above, both federal and regional state governments could play important roles, by soliciting funds for on-lending to women entrepreneurs and channelling these through the existing financial institutions. In a situation of apparent market failure, the government could create a credit guarantee programme for women entrepreneurs by mobilising resources from international financial institutions. This arrangement, already available within the extension programme for the agricultural sector, could be of immense value in overcoming the collateral requirements faced by operators in the informal economy and MSE sector in general, and women entrepreneurs in particular.

6.2.3 Access to Land and Premises

The problem of working space, sheds and premises is another area where women entrepreneurs need support. Women entrepreneurs are experiencing difficulties in meeting the high level of rents, and most of them do not own their own premises. Government, with support from donors, could establish and/or construct production and marketing sheds for women entrepreneurs in suitable locations. In order to encourage private investors to engage in the construction of suitable premises for women entrepreneurs, Government could provide incentives such as tax relief and making available plots of lease free land for productive purposes.

Once again with donor support, the Government could establish common facility centres where women entrepreneurs could undertake certain specific activities under one roof. This mechanism has the advantage of reducing costs for the individual women entrepreneurs and bringing together specialized services in a more cost-effective manner.

6.2.4 Sub-contracting Arrangements

The Government should be involved in creating an enabling environment for the implementation of subcontracting and other contractual arrangements. In this regard, incentive schemes could be provided for enterprises which engage in sub-contracting arrangements, and assistance provided for the preparation of legal/contractual arrangements with women entrepreneurs. Under such a scheme, linkages between women entrepreneurs engaged in the informal economy and the MSE sector could be better facilitated with the Women Exporters' Forum and organizations such as

COMESA. (The ILO has already had some discussions with WEF to facilitate sub-contractual linkages.)

6.3 Role of Donors and NGOs

6.3.1 Credit Facilities

Following on the proposals indicated in sections 6.1 and 6.2.2 above, it is proposed that donors and NGOs could play a crucial role in supporting MFIs and banks in providing funds that could be used for on-lending to women entrepreneurs. They may mobilize financial resources and deposit them with either MFIs or banks so that they could be channelled to women entrepreneurs, or used to create a credit guarantee programme with the financial institutions in order to minimize the women entrepreneurs' problem of lack of collateral.

Donors could also help more robust associations of women entrepreneurs to create their own financial institution (MFI) to avail special credit to their members. This approach may also help to establish the role of women entrepreneurs' associations as financial and non-financial service providers. By offering credit services, this could enable the WEAs to achieve financial sustainability and be in a stronger position to provide "credit plus" services, such as technical training and advice and lobbying support for women entrepreneurs.

6.3.2 Training and Other Capacity Building Programmes

Non-governmental organizations and donors can play a key role in mobilizing resources that could be channelled to non-financial (BDS) support service providers to enable them to carry out training needs identification programmes so that training and other support services provided are needs-based and market-oriented. Furthermore, they can assist the support service providers to organize training courses, and undertake other initiatives such as exposure visits within and outside the country so that the women entrepreneurs can exchange and learn from other experiences.

6.4 Role of Other Support Agencies

6.4.1 Credit Facilities

Non-financial (BDS) service providers could also play an important part by assuming facilitator roles and linking women entrepreneurs to credit delivery institutions. BDS providers could also play a technical intermediary role by offering the necessary training and advice on business plan preparation to women entrepreneurs, and by referring those with feasible businesses to be able to apply for credit from the MFIs and banks.

6.4.2 Marketing and Business Information Assistance

Most of the women entrepreneurs surveyed indicated marketing and business information as among the main constraints to the growth of their enterprises. To tackle this problem, various stakeholders need to address problems related to poor levels of awareness of and skills in marketing. Some of these proposed interventions are listed below.

(i) Linking Women Entrepreneurs with Medium and Large Firms

Linkages need to be created between women entrepreneurs in micro and small-scale enterprises and medium and large-scale enterprises in the form of contractual and commercial arrangements, such as through subcontracting and trading houses, which would prove to be good steps towards creating sustainable market opportunities for women entrepreneurs. In this regard, support agencies and associations could create and maintain databases of the products/services of women entrepreneurs so that they might provide a matching service with medium and large-scale enterprises. Similarly, large trading firms could be encouraged to serve as marketing outlets for the products and services of women entrepreneurs in MSEs.

(ii) Provision of Training on Quality Improvement and Cost Reduction

By monitoring those international products/services coming on to the market that may be similar to those being produced by women operators in Ethiopia, various support agencies and associations – in collaboration with the Standards and Quality Authority of Ethiopia – could provide training on quality improvement for local women entrepreneurs. This would support women entrepreneurs to ensure that they are more competitive in terms of quality, design, packaging, etc.

(iii) Market Opportunities and Appropriate/Improved Technologies

Support agencies and women entrepreneur associations (WEAs) should gather and disseminate information on existing appropriate and affordable technological options that may assist women's enterprises. Marketing information centres could be established to enable women to collect relevant market research information. The centres could be established under the Regional Micro and Small Enterprise Development Agencies (ReMSEDAs) and/or WEAs and, where these agencies or associations already exist, they could have information desks at zonal level through the zonal branches of the ReMSEDAs and/or the WEAs. In the regions where ReMSEDAs are not yet established, the information centres could be organized under Regional Trade and Industry Bureaux and/or regional WEAs.

(iv) Construction of Display Centres and Providing Advertising Support

Support agencies and/or women entrepreneur associations could initiate permanent and visible display centres with support from donors in good locations within various towns, so as to enable women entrepreneurs to display their products. The Ethiopian Women's Products Centre Emporia in Addis Ababa and those planned for other regions are potentially important steps in this regard. In addition, promotional support for the products/services of women entrepreneurs can be provided by support agencies/associations through the use of public media and by assisting women entrepreneurs to produce their own brochures, posters, advertising and promotional materials, etc.

Moreover, support agencies/associations could organize exhibitions and/or enable women entrepreneurs to participate in exhibitions and buyers/seller meetings. Special events could also be organized by support agencies/associations for the display of products/services of women entrepreneurs only. Valuable initiatives have already been undertaken by the Micro Enterprise Development Forum (MEDF) with support and assistance from the ILO's WEDGE team, as part of the ILO-Ireland Aid Partnership Programme.

6.4.3 Other Business Development Services (BDS)

Provision of other business development services such as training, both technical and managerial, as well as advisory and counselling services, can be crucial for the sustainable growth of women's enterprises. Leadership training and the development of negotiation skills could be provided for women entrepreneurs to help them build their confidence as businesswomen. In this regard, support agencies need to consider tailoring their training and advisory services to meet the specific needs and situations of women entrepreneurs. As indicated from the field survey, most women entrepreneurs are married women who also assume household responsibilities. Hence, the training packages have to be delivered at places and times convenient to women entrepreneurs. Advisory and counselling could take place at their businesses, thereby making it more convenient for the women. Training could be arranged in nearby locations which are convenient for transportation services. Support organizations can also play facilitating roles by referring and linking women entrepreneurs to other organizations for special skills training.

6.4.4 Co-ordination of Activities and Awareness Creation

The provision of services for women entrepreneurs should be better coordinated in order to increase the effectiveness of such programmes, as currently there appears to be little cooperation or coordination amongst service providers.

Thus, it is proposed that one coordinating institution for BDS services for women entrepreneurs be established at the federal and regional levels for streamlining needs-based services to women entrepreneurs. In addition, women entrepreneurs should be made more aware of the role and contributions of various support services and the availability of commercial BDS service providers and institutions. Such awareness creation could be undertaken by the information centres that it is proposed should be created in various towns. Building awareness of existing laws and regulations amongst women entrepreneurs should be considered as an important activity by the Government.

However, it is also noted that a considerable amount of effort is already going into improving collaboration and coordination among the various governmental, donor and NGO actors. The Ministry of Trade and Industry Women's Affairs Department (MTI/WAD) has been instrumental in bringing together other major players such as GTZ (and the Ethio-German MSE support programme), UNIDO, UNCTAD/EMPRETEC and the ILO to facilitate greater sharing of experiences and lessons, and to ensure more effective and efficient use of resources.

6.4.5 Capacity Building for Women's Support Agencies

The support agencies and organizations such as women entrepreneurs associations, sectoral associations, and women-related (focused) Government organizations should be supported to provide more effective services for women entrepreneurs through strengthening their institutional (human resource and material) capacities. Government, donors and women's support organizations – such as women entrepreneurs associations (WEAs), sectoral associations, Federal and Regional MSE Development Agencies, Chambers of Commerce, Women Affairs Department sof the Ministry of Trade and Industry (MTI), and Regional Trade and Industry Bureaux –

should provide training opportunities both locally and abroad to acquire experiences of similar developments in other countries. In addition, support in basic office facilities, hardware and software, would in turn add to the quality of support available for associations.

6.4.6 Monitoring and Evaluation

Monitoring and evaluation activities have to be carried out both at the level of the promotional organizations to evaluate the provision of services, and at women entrepreneurs' level to consider the impacts of services provided on their enterprises, on job creation and on poverty reduction.

6.4.7 Women Entrepreneurs' Associations

Women entrepreneurs' associations should be supported to build their own capacity and capability to provide quality services for their members. It is only if they provide real benefit for their members that they can win the confidence of the existing and potential members and create stronger and more viable associations. In November 2002, the ILO in association with MTI/WAD and in close cooperation with GTZ, provided a one-week capacity building programme for women entrepreneur associations. During 2003, it is planned that there will be 3 more capacity building programmes organized for associations of women entrepreneurs at the regional level.

6.4.8 Further Areas to be Explored

Several other areas were identified through the field survey that could be explored further. These are:
- Ways and means of enabling women entrepreneurs' associations to deliver quality services, such as BDS, to their members in a sustainable manner;
- Promotion of innovative business ideas through examining the experiences and good practices of successful women-owned businesses;
- Additional research to examine the experiences of young women (20-30 years old) in order to support them in establishing and growing their own businesses.

6.4.9 Continuing role for ILO support

The ILO should continue and upscale its support for women's entrepreneurship development in Ethiopia through the work of its WEDGE team, and with financial assistance provided under the ILO-Ireland Aid Partnership Programme.

As the objectives of ILO's Women Entrepreneurship Development and Gender Equality (WEDGE) team are to enhance the creation of meaningful employment and contribute to the reduction of poverty, the issue of men-operated micro and small enterprises has to be researched further to explore the differences between generic and gender-specific issues of MSE promotion.

7. Recommendations from the Group Work from the National Stakeholders' Conference in Addis Ababa, 19 November 2002

The ILO, in association with the MTI/WAD, organized a national conference on women's entrepreneurship at the Addis Ababa Hilton hotel on 19 November 2002. The conference was attended by more than 140 women entrepreneurs and key supporting actors. The second half of the conference was devoted to a participatory consultative process, thereby enabling participants to reflect on the findings of the field research and formulate priority actions and recommendations aimed at informing the planning processes of the ILO, MTI/WAD and other supporting agencies. The major issues and recommendations arising from the group work sessions are presented below.

7.1 Access to Resources, in particular to Finance

(a)   Issues:

- A number of background issues were identified concerning women entrepreneurs' access to appropriate resources.
- Large and micro loans are available for businesses, but there is little in the way of medium-sized loans for growth-oriented MSEs. There is a need to "fill the gap in the middle" in terms of accessing finance.
- Micro-finance institutions (MFIs) do lend money to women, but they do not provide business development services or advice. They tend to lend to micro-entrepreneurs who generally enter and operate in overcrowded market segments.
- Women entrepreneurs find it difficult to secure appropriate workspaces at reasonable rents.

(b)   Recommendations:

I. There is a need to strengthen the capacities of MFIs in order that they are better able to:
-   Extend their activities to more women as well as a wider range of women entrepreneurs;
-   Improve the coverage of their services across the country;
-   Improve their products and lending services to meet the needs of growth-oriented businesswomen by providing larger loans and longer repayment periods;
-   Review interest rates with a view to offering variable rates based on business needs.

The Government should give special emphasis to the allocation of land and premises to women entrepreneurs at reasonable rates.

II. Where market failure exists, SME development incubators need to be established to help alleviate the shortage of appropriate premises for women entrepreneurs, as well as the provision of more and better BDS and information services for women entrepreneurs.

7.2   Market Access and Developing BDS

(a)   Issues

A number of issues emerged concerning the difficulties that women entrepreneurs face in obtaining information about new market opportunities and market entry requirements, especially for export markets, where they increasingly face the economic impact of global competition.   Women also face specific challenges concerning their abilities to travel and physically access markets outside of their immediate communities.

(b)   Recommendations:

I. In the face of apparent market failure, BDS providers should consider offering assistance in marketing to facilitate women entrepreneurs' access to local, regional and international markets, and to encourage and promote the greater use of technology to achieve this.

II. The ILO should continue with its support for improving market access for women entrepreneurs through trade fairs, and continue promoting international lessons and best practices.

III. The Government and business advocacy groups should encourage links between BDS providers, MFIs and other financial institutions to improve women entrepreneurs' access to the full range of financial and non-financial (BDS) support services available.

IV. BDS products and services should be promoted to move women entrepreneurs into more profitable sectors and to help make their enterprises more productive and competitive. This should involve BDS provision in areas such as:
- Quality assurance schemes
- Productivity Improvement Programmes
- Production technology
- Product development
- Packaging development
- Business skills development
- Information about markets including export markets
- Support with information technology

7.3   Capacity Building for BDS

(a)   Issues:

The issues that emerged from the group discussions focused on the appropriateness and effectiveness of BDS provision in meeting the needs of women entrepreneurs.

(b)   Recommendations:

I. A review is needed of the existing provision of business support services (BDS): who provides BDS, and what is the current market situation for BDS in Ethiopia with particular reference to women entrepreneurs' access to and take-up/use of BDS.

II. Improve women entrepreneurs' access to resources by, for example, encouraging associations of women entrepreneurs to help their members to access BDS through referral systems.

III. Develop capacities and capabilities of BDS providers in areas such as networking, lobbying, empowerment, gender equality issues, and decision-making for women entrepreneurs.

IV. BDS providers can encourage the greater uptake of their services through cost-sharing initiatives (with WEAs and other organizations) and by providing demand-driven services.

V. BDS providers should promote the provision of integrated support across the MSE sector, and for women entrepreneurs in particular, that meets a range of client needs and avoids duplication, rather than offering a range of *ad hoc* provision of BDS.

VI. While developing more extensive and better BDS provision throughout the country, the financial sustainability of the BDS services should be a priority.

7.4   Enabling Environment

(a)   Issues:

A wide range of issues was discussed during the group work. The main points raised were as follows:

- The bureaucracy of government regulations and red tape, the largely negative attitudes towards business, and the overall lack of transparency prevent the development of a real public-private partnership for business.
- There are great differences between the laws and customary practices as regards gender equality in society, and this impacts negatively on the operations and effectiveness of women entrepreneurs.
- The licensing procedures relating to business are overly bureaucratic, and obtaining accessible information about new laws and legislation in a timely manner is a major inhibitor for business.
- Attitudes to business owners, including women entrepreneurs, are in general negative in so far as they are seen as being unethical.
- Women entrepreneurs' associations need to be supported to be more, representative, member-based, open and effective. There is a need for better networking within and between different business associations.
- The informal economy needs to be recognized in some way. It is a dominant sector in the Ethiopian economy and employs many poor people, especially

women. Poor working conditions and little income security for those engaged in the informal economy makes them very vulnerable.

(b)   Recommendations:

I. As the informal economy is largely dominated by women, it is important that steps are taken by the Government and BDS providers to improve their economic and social protection position by:

-   Providing some form of 'official' recognition to informal workers to protect them from harassment and provide basic forms of social protection;
-   Providing financial and non-financial support to women in the informal economy so that they can more easily access and navigate the steps involved in formalizing their businesses.

II. The Government should take the lead in a number of initiatives aimed at changing the attitudes of society towards women entrepreneurs and creating a more positive and constructive environment for their expansion and growth.

III. Special efforts should be made to improve partnerships between all actors who influence the socio-economic environment for women in general, and for women entrepreneurs in particular. This could be done within the framework of the PRSP process, and under the umbrella of the Women's Affairs Division, Office of the Prime Minister.

IV. There is a need to promote and support the practice of good governance by all, in government, business and non-government organizations. There is a need to highlight and reward positive, honest and transparent practices wherever and whenever they occur.

V. There is a need to promote gender equality in enterprise development through:

-   Enforcing laws in an equitable and transparent manner
-   Identifying and promoting the dissemination of good practice examples from other countries
-   Promoting women entrepreneur role models through videos films and other publicity and promotional materials.

VI. Develop women entrepreneurs' voice through advocacy and lobbying. Women entrepreneurs need to be supported and profiled in exercising their rights.

Bibliography

Barwa, S.D., 2003: *Supporting Women in Enterprise in Vietnam: Impact of Start Your Business (SYB) Training on Women Entrepreneurs in Viet Nam*, Hanoi: ILO; Geneva: IFP/SEED-WEDGE.

Barney-Gonzalez, M.J., 2002: Promoting Women's Entrepreneurship and Access to Markets Through Exhibitions and Fairs, Addis Ababa, Ethiopia, April-May 2002, IFP/SEED WEDGE; Geneva.

Bezhani, Mimoza, 2001: *Women Entrepreneurs in Albania*. Geneva: ILO, IFP/SEED-WEDGE Working Paper No. 21.

Central Statistical Authority, 1995: The 1994 Population and Housing Census of Ethiopia, Central Statistical Authority, Addis Ababa.

Central Statistical Authority, 1997: The Report on Small Scale Manufacturing Industry Survey, Central Statistical Authority, Addis Ababa

Central Statistical Authority, 1997: The Report on Urban Informal Sector Sample Survey, Central Statistical Authority, Addis Ababa

Essoo, Venda: *Promoting Female Entrepreneurship in Mauritius: Strategies in Training and Development*. Geneva: ILO, IFP/SEED-WEDGE Working Paper (forthcoming).

Ferdinand, Carol (ed.), 2001: *Jobs, Gender and Small Enterprises in the Caribbean: Lessons from Barbados, Suriname and Trinidad and Tobago*. Geneva: ILO, IFP/SEED-WEDGE Working Paper No. 19.

Goheer, Nabeel A., 2003: *Women Entrepreneurs in Pakistan: How to improve their bargaining power*. Islamabad: ILO; Geneva: IFP/SEED-WEDGE.

ILO, 2003: *Tanzanian Women Entrepreneurs: Going for Growth*. Geneva: ILO, IFP/SEED-WEDGE (forthcoming).

ILO, 2003: *Zambian Women Entrepreneurs: Going for Growth*. Geneva: ILO, IFP/SEED-WEDGE (forthcoming).

ILO, 2003: *L'entreprenariat féminine dans les îles de l'océan Indien*. Antananarivo: ILO (forthcoming).

ILO, 2002: *Promoting Women's Entrepreneurship through Employers' Organizations in the Asia-Pacific Region: Final Report. October 2002*. Geneva: ILO, IFP/SEED-WEDGE.

ILO, 2002: *Promoting Women's Entrepreneurship through Employers' Organizations in the Asia-Pacific Region: Final Report. Annexes: Presentations and Papers. October 2002*. Geneva: ILO, IFP/SEED-WEDGE.

ILO, 2002: Report of the Committee on the Informal Economy, Provisional Record (19th Session), ILO, Geneva.

JUDAI & Associates, 2002: *Jobs, Gender and Small Enterprises in Africa: Women Entrepreneurs in Zambia.* A Preliminary Report. Geneva: IFP/SEED-WEDGE, October.

Kantor, Paula, 2000: *Promoting Women's Entrepreneurship Development based on Good Practice Programmes: Some Experiences from the North to the South.* Geneva: ILO, IFP/SEED-WEDGE Working Paper No. 9.

Karim, Nilufer Ahmed, 2001: *Jobs, Gender and Small Enterprises in Bangladesh: Factors Affecting Women Entrepreneurs in Small and Cottage Industries in Bangladesh.* Geneva: ILO, IFP/SEED-WEDGE Working Paper No. 14.

Marcucci, Pamela Nichols, 2001: *Jobs, Gender and Small Enterprises in Africa and Asia: Lessons drawn from Bangladesh, the Philippines, Tunisia and Zimbabwe.* Geneva: ILO, IFP/SEED-WEDGE Working Paper No. 18.

Mayoux, Linda, 2001: *Jobs, Gender and Small Enterprises: Getting the Policy Environment Right.* Geneva: ILO, IFP/SEED-WEDGE Working Paper No. 15.

Ministry of Finance and Economic Development, 2002: Strategy Paper for Promoting Development and Poverty Reduction, MOFED, Addis Ababa.

Stoyanovska, Antonina, 2001: *Jobs, Gender and Small Enterprises in Bulgaria.* Geneva: ILO, IFP/SEED-WEDGE Working Paper No. 20.

The Federal Democratic Republic Ethiopia, 1997: Micro and Small Enterprises Development Strategy, FDRE, Addis Ababa.

University of Dar es Salaam Entrepreneurship Centre (UDEC), 2002: *Jobs, Gender and Small Enterprises in Africa: Women Entrepreneurs in Tanzania.* A Preliminary Report. Geneva, ILO, IFP/SEED-WEDGE, October.

Zewde & Associates, 2002: *Jobs, Gender and Small Enterprises in Africa: Women Entrepreneurs in Ethiopia.* A Preliminary Report, Geneva: ILO, IFP/SEED-WEDGE, October.

ANNEXES

Annex – I THE QUESTIONNAIRE

(Read the Amharic Introductory Dialogue)

Survey Questionnaire for Assessing Factors Affecting Women Entrepreneurs in Micro and Small Enterprises in Ethiopia.

Name of interviewer _____

Date of interview _____

Place of interview:

      Town:_____

      Region _____

(Read the Amharic Introductory Dialogue)

Part I Individual Level: Basic Information

1.1   Name of the respondent _____

1.2   Which age bracket are you in?

      1. Less than 20   ☐

      2. 20-39   ☐

      3. 40-49   ☐

      4. 50-59   ☐

      5. 60- above   ☐

1.3   Place of Birth _____

1.4   Marital status:

      1. Married ☐   2. Divorced ☐ 3. Separated ☐

      4. Single ☐   5. Widowed ☐

1.5   Do you have any formal education?

      1 Yes ☐   2 No ☐

1.6   If yes, to Question 1.5, highest grade completed?

      1 Primary   ☐

      2 Secondary   ☐

      3 Vocational   ☐

      4. Others (specify)_____

1.7   What professional qualifications do you have?

      1. Certificate   ☐

      2. Diploma   ☐

      3. Degree   ☐

      4. Not applicable   ☐

1.8   If No to Question1.5, do you read and write?

      1. Yes   ☐   2. No   ☐

1.9 If No to Question 1.8, who assists you in communicating for your business? (with suppliers, government offices, customers, etc.)

    1. Your husband ☐   2. Your son/daughter ☐   3. Relative ☐

    4. Friend ☐   5. Other _____

1.10 How many persons are there in your household? _____

Dependents Age	Male	Female	Total	Relation to the owner
0-4 Years				
5-18 Years				
18 Years and above				

1.11 What were you doing immediately before starting this business?

    1. Student ☐ 2 .unemployed ☐ 3 employed ☐ 4. housewife ☐

    5. Another business (specify)_____

    6. Others (specify)_____

1.12 Did you have any prior work experience relating to this business?

    1. Yes - Substantial ☐   2. Very little ☐

    3. No, just started from scratch ☐

1.13 If you had prior business experience, who owned the business?

    1. Other people ☐

    2. Myself ☐

    3. My family ☐

    4. Others, specify _____

1.14 Is the business or enterprise still operating?

    1. Yes ☐   2. No ☐

1.15 If No to Question 1.14, what was the major reason? _____

1.16 Was it a formal business?

    1. Yes ☐   2. No ☐

(To link, see the Interviewer Guide)

Part II Enterprise Level Basic Information

2.1 Name of the enterprise _____

2.2 Address: Woreda _____ Kebele _____ House No._____

    Telephone _____ Fax number _____(your own)

2.3 When did this business start (Year) _____

2.4 Who initiated the business idea?

    1. Myself ☐ 2.My husband ☐ 3.Other family member ☐

    4. Friends ☐

    5. Taken over already established business ☐

    6. Bought existing business ☐

    7. Other_____

2.5   Main product/service of the enterprise _____

2.6   What sector is your business in?

    1. Trade   ☐

    2. Production   ☐

    3. Services   ☐

    4. Hand-craft   ☐

    5. Other (specify) _____

2.7   Type of Enterprise

    1 Micro (2-5 employees) ☐   2. Small Enterprise   (above 5)   ☐

2.8   Are you engaged full-time in this business?

    1. Yes   ☐   2. No   ☐

2.9   Form of ownership

    1. Individual proprietorship   ☐

    2. Partnership   ☐

    3. Share Company   ☐

    4. Private Limited Company   ☐

    5. Others (specify)_____

2.10 Do you have a working premise?

    1. Yes   ☐   2. No   ☐

2.11 If Yes to Question 2.10, is the premise

    1. Owned? ☐   2. Rented?   ☐   3. Other? (Specify) _____

2.12 How many employees do you have?

Type of employment	Female	Male
Full time		
Part time		
Paid family members		
Unpaid family members		

(To link, see the Interviewer Guide)

Part III Information on Entrepreneurial Capacity, Resources for start up

3.1   Why did you prefer to start your own business?

    1. Family tradition   ☐   4. Small investment is required   ☐

    2. To be self-employed ☐   5. No other alternative for incomes   ☐

    3. Brings high income   ☐   6. Others

3.2 What were the responses of your spouse & other family members when you started your enterprise?

Category	Very supportive	Supportive	Indifferent	Not supportive	Reacted badly
Spouse					
Other Family Members					

3.3 What were the three most motivating factors to start this business?

1_____

2_____

3_____

3.4 What equipment or other assets did you have (have access to) when starting/creating the enterprise? _____

3.5 How were these obtained?

1. Purchased ☐   2. Leased/granted ☐ 3. Inherited ☐

4. Other (specify)_____

3.6 How much did it cost you to set up the business? (ETB Birr) _____ ____

3.7 What was your main source of start-up funding?

1. Personal saving ☐
2. household ☐
3. Borrowed from relatives or friends/money lenders ☐
4. Micro-finance institutions ☐
5. Equb ☐
6. Assistant from friends/relatives ☐
7. Inheritance ☐
8. Borrowed from Bank ☐
9. Assistant from NGO's ☐
10. Others (specify) _____

3.8 Do you get support with household chores/childcare (like nursery and schools, day care centres, formalized or not).

1 Yes ☐   2 No ☐

3.9 What support did you get to start this business?

1. Government Policies ☐
2. Easy access to credit ☐
3. Financial support from relatives/friends ☐
4. Material support from relatives/friends ☐
5. Both financial and non-financial support from relatives/friends ☐
6. None ☐

3.10 What were the five greatest constraints you faced at establishment?

(DO NOT READ ANSWERS)'

    1. Working space   ☐

    2. Working capital/finance   ☐

    3. Support services that would build my confidence   ☐

    4. Appropriately skilled labour   ☐

    5. Obtaining the licences etc.   ☐

    6. Access to raw materials   ☐

    7. Government rules and regulations   ☐

    8. Lack of credit facilities   ☐

    9. Others _____

3.11 How did you overcome these problems? _____

3.12 Did you get any external formal support services?

    1. Yes   ☐   2 No   ☐

3.13 If Yes to Q.3.12, what type of support?

    1.   Financial   ☐   2.   Technical   ☐

    3.   Managerial   ☐   4.   Market information   ☐

    5.   Networking   ☐   6.   Other coaching   ☐

3.14 How were these types of supports accessed? _____

(To link, see the Interviewer Guide)

3.15 Who decides on how the enterprise money is utilized?

    1. My husband   ☐   2. Myself   ☐

    3. Other members of the family ☐   99 don't know   ☐

3.16 Who is responsible in your business for making major decisions?

    1. Myself ☐   2. My husband ☐   3. Other family members ☐

    4. Friends Jointly with my husband ☐   5. Other (specify)_____

3.17 Where do you sell most of your products/services?

    1. Local market - area of work/residence   ☐

    2. Regional markets - capital city of the regional state   ☐

    3. National markets - Addis Ababa   ☐

    4. Foreign market - outside Ethiopia   ☐

3.18 How do you sell or promote your products/services?

    1. Marketed directly by the company itself   ☐

    2. Through an intermediary   ☐

    3. Production is based on demand   ☐

    4. Sold to retailers   ☐

3.19 Do you promote your products/services?

    1. Yes   ☐   2. No   ☐

3.20 If Yes to question 3.19, then how?

    1. By word of mouth   ☐

    2. Local news paper   ☐

3. Exhibition ☐

4. Radio ☐

5. Television ☐

6. Other (specify)_____

3.21 What are the three major marketing constraints of your business?

1 _____

2 _____

3 _____

3.22 What type of decision(s) is (are) difficult for you? _____

3.23 Do you keep your enterprise money separate from your personal money?

1 Yes ☐ 2 No ☐

3.24 Do you keep records of your costs in order to calculate your profit?

1 Yes ☐ 2 No ☐

3.25 Do you pay yourself a wage/salary?

1. Yes ☐ 2. No ☐

3.26 If No to Question 3.25, then why? _____

3.27 How much is your salary on a regular basis? _____

(**To link, see the Amharic guide**)

Part IV Information on the Level of Development/Diversification of Enterprise

4.1 Have you developed, diversified, expanded, and changed your enterprise since establishment?

1 Yes ☐ 2 No ☐

4.2 If Yes to Question 4.1, in what way?

1. Expanded size of the enterprises ☐

2. Added new products ☐

3. Hired more workers ☐

4. Improved quality of the product ☐

5. Reduced costs by buying inputs in bulk ☐

6. Reduced costs with cheaper source of credit ☐

7. Started selling in new markets ☐

8. Changed the type of business ☐

9. Reduced the type of products ☐

10. Reduced number of employees ☐

11. Reduced market outlet ☐

12. Relocated working premises ☐

13. Others(Specify)_____

4.3 Has there been any temporary closure of your business in the last two years?

1 Yes ☐ 2 No ☐

4.4 If Yes to Q. 4.3 why? _____

4.5   How did you get the skills to diversify and develop your business?

       1. By training   ☐   2. By advice ☐   3. Own experience ☐

       4. Other (Specify) _____

4.6   Do you feel you are successful in your business?

       1 Yes   ☐   2 No   ☐

4.7   If Yes to Question 4.6, how? _____

4.8   If No to Question 4.6, why? _____

4.9   How do you measure growth of your enterprise? (Probe by asking) _____

       (To link, see the Interviewer Guide)

Part V Information on Business Enabling Environment, Facilities/Resources Available

5.1   Are you aware of the following government policies?

       1. Proclamation on Trade registration and licensing   ☐

       2. National Micro and Small Enterprise (MSE) Strategy   ☐

       3. Micro-finance Institution Proclamation   ☐

       4. National Policy on Ethiopian Women   ☐

5.2   Do you think the present policy environment discriminates against women?

       1. Yes ☐   2. No   ☐

5.3   If your answer to Q. 5.2 is yes, in what way and level?

       1. In its content and meaning   ☐   2. At implementation level   ☐

       3. The fact that it is gender neutral   ☐

5.4   If your answer to Q. 5.2 is No, in what way?

       1. In its content and meaning   ☐   2. At implementation level ☐

       3. The fact that it is gender neutral   ☐

5.5   Do you think changes in government policies would help women's enterprise to grow?

       1. Yes ☐   2. No ☐

5.6   If your answer is yes to Q5.5, what policies and why? _____

5.7   If your answer is no to Q5.5, why?_____

5.8   Are you aware of government regulations affecting your business?(Don't

       read: labour law, tax, safety and health, licensing, others)

       1. Yes ☐   2. No ☐

5.9   If your answer is yes to Q.5.8, have you tried to comply with those regulations?

       1. Yes ☐   2. No ☐

5.10 What problems did you face to comply with the

       regulations?_____

5.11 What are your current sources of finance for the business now?

       1.   Money lenders   ☐

       2.   Credit in kind   ☐

       3.   Credit from micro-finance institutions   ☐

       4.   Bank loan   ☐

       5.   Ploughing back   ☐

6.   back the profit ☐

7.   Others (specify) _____

5.12 Are you affiliated with business and/or women's organizations ?

    1 Yes   ☐   2 No   ☐

5.13 If Yes to Q. 5.12, how do you see the role of such organizations in promoting women's

    enterprises? _____

5.14 Which are the organizations you are affiliated with? _____

5.15 Are you aware of institutions that give support to business growth and those with special facilities

    for women?

Services rendered	Aware	Not aware
1. Saving and credit services		
2. Indirect credit services (feasibility & application processing, technical advice etc.)		
3. Marketing assistance		
4. Technology assistance		
5. Provision of extension services		
6. Training in small business management, etc		
7. Business information		
8. Networking		
9. Others (Specify)		

(To link, see the Interviewer Guide)

VI. Information on Current Problems and Prospects

6.1   Given the trend in your business performance do you expect to be in the same business five

    years from now?

    1 Yes   ☐   2 No   99 don't know

6.2   If No to Q.6.1 Why? _____

6.3   If Yes to Q.6.1, why?_____

6.4   What were the three biggest obstacles you face in developing/doing

    business? (do not read but probe)

    1.   lack of skill in negotiation ☐

    2.   lack of confidence to take riskier business ☐

    3.   lack of adequate working capital ☐

    4.   problem of mobility as a result of household chores ☐

    5.   lack of managerial skill

        (record keeping, marketing, project idea generation etc.) ☐

    6.   lack of support from the rest of the household members ☐

        (husband, children etc.)

    7.   problem of working space or sales outlet ☐

    8.   others (Specify) _____

6.5 How did you over come these obstacles? _____

6.6 Can you mention specific changes in the business environment now (recently, since Government promised to implement certain measures to assist women entrepreneurs)?

    1 Yes ☐   2 No ☐

6.7 If Yes to Q.6.6 mention the specific changes? _____

6.8 Are you proud that you are self-employed?

    1 Yes ☐   2 No ☐

6.9 If someone offered you a permanent job would you give up your business? and go for the job?

    1 Yes ☐   2 No ☐

6.10 If your answer to Q. 6.9 is yes, Why?_____.

6.11 If your answer to Q.6.9 is no, why?_____

6.12 Do you have plans for the future of your enterprise?

    1 Yes ☐   2 No ☐

6.13 If your answer is yes to Q.6.12, in what areas?

    1. Expanding the business   ☐

    2. Improving the product quality   ☐

    3. Changing the type of business   ☐

    4. Penetrate new market   ☐

    5. Diversify the product/service   ☐

    6. Close the business down   ☐

    7. Improve my managerial skill   ☐

    8. Others (specify)_____

       If your answer to Q. 6.12 is no, why not? _____

    9. Observation of the Interviewer:_____

VII. Information concerning Gender

7. 1 Are there any problems, that you felt were related to being a woman?

    1 Yes   ☐

    2 No   ☐

7.2 If yes, what are they?   _____

7.3 Do you think there are major business issues/constraints you face because you are a woman entrepreneur?

    1 Yes   ☐

    2 No   ☐

7.4 If yes, mention some of them: _____

Annex 2 – List of Persons Contacted

No.	Name of Persons Contacted	Position Held	Location	Telephone
1	Ato Mitiku Ayele	Deputy Head, Bureau of Trade Industry Transport and Tourism	Awassa	(06) 20 04 18
2	W/ro. Beletu Sima	Team Leader, Trade Promotion Bureau of TITT	Awassa	(06) 20 13 48
3	Ato Degefu Tibbo	Department Head, Sidama Zone, Trade Industry, Transport and Tourism	Awassa	(06) 20 09 28
4	W/ro. Shwaye Kassahun	Expert, Bureau of Women's Affairs, SNNPRS	Awassa	(06) 20 13 96 (06) 20 40 06
5	Ato Girma Molla	Expert, TITT Bureau	Awassa	(06) 20 35 21 (06) 20 13 48
6	W/ro. Amsale Negash	Chair Person, Women Entrepreneurs Association, SNNPRS	Awassa	(06) 20 51 11
7	Ato Yitbarek Tsigie	Head, MSEs Promotion Department Bureau of Trade Industry and Tourism	Addis Ababa	(01) 56 24 86
8	Ato Demnissie Kifle	Zone 4 Trade Industry and Tourism Bureau, A.A. City Administration	Addis Ababa	(01) 15 56 15
9	W/ro Wozema Teka	Section Head, Trade Registration and Licensing, Zone 2, A.A TIT Bureau	Addis Ababa	(01) 51 37 16
10	W/ro. Atsede H/Gebriel	Office Head, Woreda 20 Trade Industry and Tourism	Addis Ababa	(01) 51 37 16
11	W/ro. Debritu Molla	Office Head, Woreda 7, Trade Industry and Tourism.	Addis Ababa	(01) 13 82 29
12	Ato Fasika Jiffar	Head Amhara ReMSEDA	Bahir Dar	(08) 20 69 76
13	Ato Assefa Taye	President of Bahir Dar Chamber of Commerce	Bahir Dar	(08) 20 32 10
14	W/ro Ashagem Belay	President of Amhara Region Women Entrepreneurs Association	Bahir Dar	(08) 20 18 00
15	W/ro Tafesuh Egezew	President of Bahir Dar Women Entrepreneurs Association	Bahir Dar	(08) 20 11 26
16	Ato Daniel Mulualem	Head Tigray ReMSEDA	Mekelle	(04) 40 89 72

17	Ato Yoseph Tesfaye	Head Tigray Trade & Industry Bureau	Mekelle	(04) 40 67 35
18	W/ro Leilty Abay	V/President of Mekelle Women Entrepreneurs Association	Mekelle	(04) 40 25 81
19	Ato Zerbrook Berhe	Secretary General, Mekelle Chamber of Commerce	Mekelle	(04) 40 25 29
20	W/ro Abeba G/Selassie	President of Mekelle Women Entrepreneurs Association	Mekelle	(04) 40 03 44
21	Ato Yetbarek Tsigie	Dept. Head MSE Development A.A Trade & Industry Bureau	Addis Ababa	(01) 56 24 86
22	Ato Abebe Negash	Manager, FeMSEDA	Addis Ababa	(01) 51 11 22
23	W/ro Tadelech Debele	Project Officer Ethiopian Women Development Fund	Addis Ababa	(01) 52 47 13
24	Ato Tesfaye	Ethiopian Women Dev't Fund	Addis Ababa	(01) 53 58 66
25	Dr. Taye Berhanu	Secretary, Ethiopian Employers Federation	Addis Ababa	(01) 52 34 19
26	Dr. Wolday Amha	Association of Ethiopian Micro Finance Institutions(AEM FI)	Addis Ababa	(01) 50 38 29
27	W/ro Achamyelesh Ashenefi	President A.A. Women Entrepreneurs Association	Addis Ababa	(01) 62 20 55
28	W/ro Nigist Haile	Head Women Affairs Department, Ministry of Trade & Industry	Addis Ababa	(01) 51 80 25
29	Ato Fantahu Melles	Head GTZ - MSE Development Programme	Addis Ababa	(01) 62 61 35
30	Ato Teshome Sileshie	Research and Promotion team leader, Trade Transport Industry and Tourism Office (TTIT)	Dire Dawa	
31	W/ro Etagegn Hailu	Research and Promotion Expert, TTIT Office	Dire Dawa	
32	Ato Ahmed Mohamed	TTIT Manager	Dire Dawa	
33	Ato Getu Haile		Nazareth	
34	W/ro Tenaye Bezabish		Nazareth	